faith Is Stranger Than fiction

faith Is Stranger Than fiction

Steve Halliday

New Leaf Press

First printing: January 2001

ISBN: 0-89221-496-1
Library of Congress Catalog Number: 00-102658

Cover by Left Coast Design, Portland, Oregon

Printed in the United States of America

Please visit our website for other great titles:
www.newleafpress.net

For information regarding publicity for author interviews contact Dianna Fletcher at (870) 438-5288.

Dedication

To the Rev. Wendell and Betty Boyer,
who taught me what a life of faith is all about.

Contents

Introduction

What's So Strange About Faith?

faith means "believing in advance what will make sense only in reverse." Those were the provocative words that stared out at us last Sunday when my wife and I joined some friends for church. The stimulating sentence greeted worshipers from its projected position at the front of the auditorium.

I think they got it just right.

God calls His people to live by faith, to place our full trust in His love and faithfulness and power and wisdom. In practice, this often means that our Lord wants us to take a step away from actions that the world considers "logical" and "prudent" and "seemly," and instead trust Him to work things out in unexpected ways that better glorify Him.

In other words, faith is stranger than fiction.

Just when we think we know how God must work in a given situation, He does something completely unanticipated. Just when we expect to see His hand move in one place, it appears somewhere else. Just when we think we would be satisfied with "A," He swoops down in response to our faith and gives us the whole alphabet — including those peculiar letters "Q" and "Z."

> "I tell you the truth," Jesus replied, "no one who has left home or brothers or sisters or mother or father or children or fields for me and the gospel will

fail to receive a hundred times as much in this present age (homes, brothers, sisters, mothers, children and fields — and with them, persecutions) and in the age to come, eternal life. But many who are first will be last, and the last first" (Mark 10:29–31).

Faith really is stranger than fiction — far more unpredictable, wonderful, thrilling, mysterious, and fiercely puzzling than we usually expect. That's not to say, of course, that those with the most faith act in the most bizarre ways. This little book does not advocate searching for the Messiah in the folds of a hot tortilla, nor does it encourage anyone to act foolishly and so to dishonor the name of the Lord. What it does aim to do is to remind all of us that God responds marvelously to the faith of His people, but He does so in ways that can't be predicted.

The surprising truth is that the Lord loves to take Satan's best shots and deflect them straight back into his devilish midsection. Our Lord seems to delight in transforming what looks like a clear victory for Satan into a stunning triumph for God's people.

In fact — if I can say such a thing without getting into trouble — at times God acts almost, well, *puckishly*. He not only brings good out of evil, He turns evil on its head. He not only triumphs over the outrage, He turns it inside out. He transforms the devil's deadliest bullets into Satan-seeking missiles. God loves to use the most unlikely scenarios to honor His children's faith by displaying His own omnipotence and the powerlessness of His enemies.

Even in the midst of tragedy, you may see a sudden stab of light through the clouds . . . an inexplicable reversal of circumstances . . . a fragile flower of matchless beauty pushing its way through the rubble and devastation. Once you start looking for the distinctive fingerprints of God Almighty, this dark, sometimes turbulent life will never look the same. God is often exactly where you do not expect to see Him, bringing good out of bad and turning evil inside out.

When our world is caving in, when things look as grim as they possibly can, when it seems as though Satan has applied the *coup de grace* to our fondest hopes and greatest desires — at precisely that point the Strong One steps in as a response to our faith and brandishes the very evil for His glory.

Now, *that* is a God to worship! *That* is a God to adore!

And that is the God who calls His people to trust Him, and who honors their faith with displays of power and wisdom that leave the angelic hosts gaping in wonder.

In this book I will try to show *how* faith is stranger than fiction. Half of the book travels all over the world to tell the remarkable stories of people of faith and how God responded to their confidence in Him. The other half investigates what the Bible has to say about the many (and often surprising!) ways in which God responds to the faith of His people. The two halves work together. The first part of each chapter offers contemporary examples of how God loves to honor believing faith, while the second part looks for corresponding patterns in the Scripture. Some readers may want to read the story portion of the chapter, then continue with the corresponding Bible-based part. Others may want to read all the story portions first, then go back and read all the biblical material. Either method will work, since all chapters are designed to stand on their own.

Although I'm no travel agent, I would like to send you on a fabulous trip to bask in a place where bright skies and subtropical winds can thaw out the most frozen of souls. A place where icy blasts get turned into balmy breezes. Where snowdrifts blocking the door become sand dunes accenting the pool.

I'd like to send you to the land where faith is stranger than fiction.

As you focus your attention on the surprising way God responds to the faith of His beloved children, you, too, may see your worst nightmares fade and vanish into the shadows. You, too, may be surprised at the unorthodox ways God honors our faith.

But then again, it shouldn't really surprise us. For both experience and His Word teach us that faith is stranger than fiction.

I

A Weaver of Extremes

Imagine that you are leading a group of 12 American high schoolers on a short-term mission trip. Then imagine you are stranded at a ranger station in the wilds of Kenya. Imagine further that darkest night has fallen. Finally, imagine that as you begin to wonder how your students might react to their perilous circumstances, you spy this poster tacked to the wall of the compound you are nervously pacing:

MEMO: REGARDING THE
TRANSPORTATION OF DEAD EMPLOYEES

If you are Rob Shafar, you don't have to imagine it. You *lived* it — in THX and Dolby stereo.

A few years ago Rob led a mission trip to Kenya to allow students from his church both to see what "real" missions looked like and to assist some hardworking missionaries. One day the group planned to make a four-hour drive from Buffalo Springs Tented Camp in the Samburu to Oruz in the Pokot. But a four-hour African drive doesn't much resemble a four-hour trip in the States. Rob likens many of Kenya's roads to "your worst driveway gone bad."

Just a few miles out of Buffalo Springs a tire on the group's minivan blew out. Rob and company had to wait with the van while their missionary hosts left to retrieve another tire. Several hours later the group once again was lumbering down the "high-way," but after another 20 miles, a second tire blew.

This time the missionaries left Rob and his group at a ranger station while they took off to scrounge another tire. "Some time after they left us," Rob said, "it occurred to me that they drove off with all our money, with all our passports, and with the only people who really knew where we were. *What if they don't come back?* I wondered. *What if they get stuck somewhere — not too improbable in Kenya — and don't return for a day or two? What am I going to do with 12 high school students on a Kenyan ranger station that was created primarily to shoot poachers?*

Trying to mask his concern, Rob began to wander around the station, looking for something to read. That's when his eye spotted the oversized memo tacked to the wall. Rob shook his head, wondering how big a problem dead employees actually presented. Fortunately, none of his students saw the notice and after a few more hours his group got underway once more. But before they traveled very far, yet another tire disintegrated, and they began the now-familiar drill.

That evening, after a man tried to sell the group his daughter, Rob and his students made camp. Everyone set out his or her things and Rob lit a campfire. A few minutes later, a vehicle stuffed with about 30 Kenyans dropped by to suggest the American group might not want to remain in that particular spot. It seems that herds of elephants liked to use that route for night-time migrations.

About 1:00 a.m. the missionaries returned. They had taken a little longer than expected, they said, because they decided to pick up a second tire, just in case. Good thing. Between the time they left and the time they returned, yet *another* tire on the minivan gave up the ghost.

If I stay here much longer, Rob must have thought, *I'm going to buy stock in Goodyear.* When the group finally arrived at Oruz later that day, seven tires in all had gone belly up.

Now most students of that age would have grown testy. But these students had already learned on this trip that God always has a purpose behind everything He does, even when you haven't a clue what it might be. So immediately after arriving in Oruz they sought out Art Davis, the missionary scheduled to pick them up. "Tell us," they asked, "why did God delay us? What was He doing here?"

"It's interesting you should ask," Art replied. "When I arrived at the station to pick you up, you weren't here. But somebody else was."

Art looked around at the group. "I've spent the past several hours talking to a man who for many years has been openly hostile to the gospel. Before our 'chance meeting' at the station, he simply did not want to hear about Christ. But today . . . today he *listened*. For hours. Perhaps that explains your seven flat tires; had you arrived on time, I would have missed a golden opportunity to speak to that man about the Lord."

Better Than the Funnies

Stories like this one convince me that faith really is stranger than fiction. Just when Satan thinks he's masterminded a foolproof plot to devastate the saints, the Lord steps out of the shadows to reveal how *His* battle plan uses even the evil scheme to lift God's children to smashing victory.

I'm convinced that if you wrap your mind around this idea, it will change the way you live. Tough circumstances and devastating blows will no longer retain the power to hold you in their grip. Sure, you'll still hurt — that's part of being human, and no book can change that — but you'll be able to look beyond the pain and hurt. You'll know to strain your eyes out toward the horizon, to fix your gaze in hope, to search for and fully anticipate what such a strange faith might do on *your* behalf.

I was forcefully reminded of this principle years ago while editing Herbert Schlossberg's intriguing book *Called to Suffer, Called to Triumph*. The author wrote about a church in Oriente, Cuba, which for years had asked permission from the Communist government to expand its facilities. After many refusals, the government changed its mind and the church knocked down the walls. At just that point the government reversed its earlier ruling and banned all further construction. That left the little Oriente church with nothing but a shell of a facility. If you were keeping a scorecard, it would certainly have seemed an obvious point for Satan.

Not quite.

The author's next words sounded so much like the strange way God works in response to the faith of His people, I almost laughed out loud:

> But the Lord has used the situation in an interesting way. Since the building has no walls the preaching and hymns are heard in the neighborhood much more clearly than if the church had been enclosed. More people are hearing the gospel this way.[1]

How like God! He takes what appear to be clear victories for the devil and turns them on their head. He uses events that threaten to deflate our confidence in Him and instead uses them to increase our faith. He works "in strange ways His wonders to perform."

In a word, God delights to show that faith is stranger than fiction. He loves to display His power on behalf of those who have entrusted their souls to His Son, the Lord Jesus Christ. If that describes you, you can live with the strong hope that God intends to build *your* faith through the delightful surprises He brings out of His heavenly warehouse.

Surprises especially reserved for *you*.

At the center of His Thoughts

I'm willing to bet, however, that some who read this chapter doubt that any such thing could ever happen in *their* case. Maybe that someone is you. Your situation has grown too desperate. Too dark. Too grim. It's been festering so long and has sunk so deep that months ago you abandoned any hope of rescue. Yes, God may love to honor the faith of others in strange, quirky ways — but He doesn't have any surprises in store for you.

Does that describe you? If so, will you at least suspend your disbelief for the time it takes to read this book? While I can't guarantee that God will turn around your situation in some gloriously odd way, I do know that, if you are His child, you live at the center of His thoughts. Your name is engraved on the very palms of His hands (Isa. 49:15–16) and He loves you with infinite passion. One day He will wipe away all your pain and tears and you will bask forever in the limitless goodness and grace of Almighty God. You will share an eternal inheritance with Jesus and will taste divine pleasures forevermore.

"Aha!" you may say, "I knew it. You're telling me the only real hope I have is found in the world to come, so I might as well get used to my dungeon in this one."

No, that's not even close to what I'm saying. I said I can't *guarantee* that God will honor your faith in some strangely wonderful way — but I think the likelihood is, He will.

In fact, I think it's safe to say that the darker the situation, the more likely it is that God will pull His rabbit out of the hat, or better, that He will turn a wolf into a rabbit!

Why? Because God's astonishing ability to bring good out of evil shows more clearly than anything else who rules the universe. The worst situations provide the best stages for the Lord to work His strange wonders.

So please, take heart! While God alone chooses when and how He will respond to our faith, desperate situations seem made-to-order for His surprises. And when they happen, you'll be left breathless.

Just as others already have discovered.

In God's Bermuda Triangle

Much has been written about the mysteries of the Bermuda Triangle, a vaguely triangular patch of ocean stretching from the southern U.S. coast to Bermuda to the Greater Antilles. According to legend, ships disappear without a trace, airplanes vanish, UFOs zip in and out of the region, and bizarre events occur there with chilling regularity.

Regardless of the truth of these reports, it is certain that for the past few years one corner of the triangle has witnessed some extraordinary events. God appears to be in the midst of honoring His people's faith in some very peculiar ways.

Cuba — that bastion of communism in the Western Hemisphere, that nation which made it hard for the church in Oriente — is opening up to the gospel.

One witness came away from a visit to Cuba, astonished at what he saw:

Everyone in Cuba is awake — not converted, but awake — and searching for God. I saw unsaved people run up to Christians and ask to be led to Christ. I saw this happen! This kind of thing has taken place before in the world. It has happened in American history, too. But it has never appeared around me.[2]

He's not alone in his amazement. Another observer filed the following report:

Just six years ago, churches in Cuba were languishing under Fidel Castro's regime of fear and intimidation. Only a few older people were willing to be identified as Christians, and they felt isolated and forgotten by the rest of the world. Bibles were scarce, religious broadcasting was not permitted, and Castro was still attempting to turn his impoverished island nation into an atheistic paradise.

Today, although Castro remains in power, the tables have turned. A religious resurgence is sweeping the country, Bible sales are booming, and thousands of new believers are filling up Pentecostal, Baptist, and Catholic churches. After loosening the ban on religion last year, Castro recently admitted he made a mistake when he tried to force atheism on his people.[3]

No wonder the old dictator thinks he made a mistake! Spontaneous meetings of Christians now occur at all hours of the day and night. One three-week evangelistic campaign resulted in 22,000 professions of faith in Christ. More Bibles were distributed in 1991–1992 than in the previous 30 years, and some observers claim informal house churches now outnumber traditional congregations by three to one. Young people flock to churches and people are more open to the gospel than perhaps ever before. "Churches that used to be half-full are having services three or four times a day," said one source. "Young people who have been indoctrinated by communism are seeing the power of God in the church."

Faith really *is* stranger than fiction! Try to close down a church in Oriente by wrecking its facilities? Fine. More people will come to the Lord that way. Try to force atheism on a people who don't want it? Fine. In the end, they will stampede to hear the gospel.

Of course, you don't have to travel to Cuba to see how God loves to honor the faith of His people — yet in strange and unexpected ways. Examples abound.

Vera Mae Perkins, the wife of evangelist and social activist John Perkins, knows firsthand how God's answers to prayer outstrip the imagination of the best novel writer. After describing the beatings her husband took in Mississippi jails, how motels refused her family service because of race, and how difficult it could be to rear eight kids on little money, she writes:

> Our struggles were painful, but I grew to expect them and — believe it or not — even appreciate them. Many young couples, especially wives, believe that suffering should be avoided at all costs — that God wouldn't want them or their children to suffer. Although this is a natural inclination, it is very far from the truth. Suffering builds character and faith. Many times God calls us to a life that includes suffering. John and I find that suffering together through hard times makes us depend on each other more, and binds us closer together.[4]

I thought the devil intended suffering to crush the faith of God's people. Yet what have we here? God can use even suffering to increase His people's faith.

Pretty strange.

Joanne Shetler, a missionary with Wycliffe Bible Translators to the Balangao people of the Philippines, has seen some pretty strange responses to her faith, as well. What God does can be so surprising, so unusual, so divine that we never see it coming.

Happily, however, we can rejoice once the muck has cleared from our eyes!

For many months, Shetler had longed for the Balangao Christians to grow past their short, perfunctory prayers. In the middle of the night she would wake up and beg God to teach these new believers to pray. She then uttered a desperate prayer herself. "God," she said, "I don't care what you have to do; make these people pray!"

A dangerous prayer when addressed to a God who loves strange answers!

Some time later Shetler and Dr. Robespierre Lim were flying back to the remote village in a helicopter loaded with supplies earmarked for the Balangao's first hospital. On descent they hit a tree and crashed. Shetler suffered severe injuries and began to panic when she realized their awful extent. But real terror filled her heart when she thought she might die before she could finish translating the Bible into the language of her friends.

As fuel spilled from a big gash in the craft and flames leapt all around, Shetler heard voices yelling to get back, that the helicopter was about to explode. When the Balangaos realized Shetler was alive and still inside, however, they rushed back to the burning wreck, doused the craft with mud and water, and snuffed out the flames.

Shetler's rescuers turned their heads when they got their first glimpse of her: broken ribs, one collapsed lung, eyes filled with powdered cement. The caustic lime in the cement ate into soft tissue and caused her eyes to feel as if they had burst into flame. Some villagers thought her condition hopeless: "Can't you see she's already dead — just her breath is left."

But faith really is stranger than fiction. In fact, God was about to spring a mountain-sized surprise on the Balangao people. And on Shetler.

The night was long, the pain intense. But something else was going on. Something new for Balangaos. One by one, throughout the night, Balangao Christians worked their way through the throng, touched my hand, and prayed. I'll never forget their prayers: "God, don't let her die, the Book's not done yet. Just let her live; the Book's not done yet."

That night, as I lay on the floor, more dead than alive, the Balangaos were praying — really praying. One after another, they prayed the same prayer, "Don't let her die, the Book's not done yet."

It was the worst and best night of my life all wrapped up in one. The worst pain I'd ever known was eclipsed by moments of indescribable awe over their prayers. Only God could weave such extremes.[5]

That's the secret! "Only God can weave such extremes." Only God can take the extremes of your life — the desperate and the delightful — and craft them into surprises of faith too exquisite for words. Only God can do that! In a snap. In the twinkle of His eye.

Why? Because He loves to respond to even a tiny flicker of faith with mighty acts that leave us in awe. And that's true in Kenya, in Cuba, in Mississippi, in the Philippines . . . in fact, wherever His kids live.

And that includes your address, too.

Insight from the Bible

In this book I repeatedly make the claim that faith is stranger than fiction. I don't expect you to take my word for it, however. In fact, I wouldn't want you to. Scripture is full of incidents which illustrate this delightful principle. For this chapter, however, allow me to focus on just two biblical accounts, one from each testament.

Losers of the Raided Ark

In the days before Israel crowned its first king, war raged between the Hebrews and the Philistines. About four thousand Israelites died in a fierce battle described in 1 Samuel 4. The disaster prompted Israel's terrified elders to order that the ark of the covenant be brought out from its resting place in Shiloh and carried to the front lines. The ark, you'll remember, was a large wooden box overlaid with gold, its solid gold cover decorated with two mighty angels, their strong wings extended toward each other. In the ark lay a copy of the Ten Commandments, Aaron's rod that budded, and the hopes of Israel.

The frightened Hebrew leaders committed the same error Hollywood made in its blockbuster, *Raiders of the Lost Ark*. They assumed that the box itself would confer irresistible power. They couldn't imagine that God would allow the box to be taken hostage. Somehow they had forgotten that the ark was merely a shadow, a symbol, of the awesome holiness and might of God himself. The Israelites foolishly expected the presence of the box to give them victory.

When the Philistines heard that the ark had arrived in the Israelite camp, they too fell prey to superstition — but only for awhile. They said:

> "A god has come into the camp," they said. "We're in trouble! Nothing like this has happened before. Woe to us! Who will deliver us from the hand of these mighty gods? They are the gods who struck the Egyptians with all kinds of plagues in the desert. Be strong, Philistines! Be men, or you will be subject to the Hebrews, as they have been to you. Be men, and fight! (1 Sam. 4:7–9).

The Philistines did fight, and they won. In the ensuing battle, thirty thousand Israelite foot soldiers perished. The two sons of the high priest, Eli, died — and the ark itself was seized as spoils of war. As chapter 4 draws to a close, the scene looks impossibly dark. Eli dies after hearing of the disastrous battle, and his daughter-in-law quickly follows him after giving premature birth to a son. The chapter ends with these dismal words:

> Then she murmured, "Name the child 'Ichabod,' for Israel's glory is gone." (Ichabod means "there is no glory." She named him this because the Ark of God had been captured and because her husband and her father-in-law were dead) (1 Sam. 4:21–22; TLB).

In all of Israel's long, checkered history, it's hard to find a more somber scene.

Meanwhile, the Philistines exulted. Danced. Partied. Slapped high fives. Not only had they crushed Israel in battle, but events had proven their gods stronger than the God of the Jews.

Or so they thought.

Such a deduction would have seemed logical in the world of the ancient Near East. If you won a battle, that meant your gods were stronger than the opposition's. So it seemed as though Yahweh, the God of Israel, showed his true weakness — He was no more than a two-bit deity for losers.

The Philistines took the ark and set it up as a trophy in the temple of their own god, Dagon, and went to sleep with dreams of sweet conquest. Then the morning dawned, and with it a shock — Dagon had fallen on his face before the ark!

Supposing this to be an unfortunate accident (but possibly a bit ill-at-ease), the Philistines set Dagon back in his place. But the next morning, they found their fish god licking dust once again — this time, with his head and hands broken off and lying on the threshold. A chill swept the populace.

They didn't know it, but God had just begun a classic demonstration that faith is stranger than fiction.

This odd nighttime event soon exploded into a daytime nightmare. A plague broke out among the inhabitants of Ashdod, where the ark had been taken, and the people instantly recognized its cause: "The ark of the god of Israel must not stay here with us, because his hand is heavy upon us and upon Dagon our god," they said (1 Sam. 5:7).

So they did what any good pagan would do: they sent the ark to their unsuspecting neighbors. The plague soon followed.

After brief appearances in Ashdod, Gath, and Ekron, the Philistines had suffered enough.

So they summoned the mayors again and begged them to send the Ark back to its own country, lest the entire city die. For the plague had already begun and great fear was sweeping across the city. Those who didn't die were deathly ill; and there was weeping everywhere (1 Sam. 5:11–12;TLB).

Following seven months of misery, the Philistines returned the ark to Israel, laden with golden offerings. They did this to "pay honor to Israel's God," hoping that He would lift His hand from them and their gods and their land (1 Sam. 6:5). At last they had learned their puny gods were no match for the Lord of all the earth — not even when a military triumph appeared to suggest otherwise.

Let's not miss what this story teaches. Israel's defeat in battle *was* a dreadful thing; there's no doubt about that. And it is certain that the capture of the ark marked a low point in the Jewish nation's history. Without question, the surrounding Gentile peoples reasoned that Israel's defeat and the seizure of God's ark meant Dagon could whip Yahweh.

But God took that very evil and turned it on its head. For the sake of His name and for the sake of the beleaguered, believing remnant who still worshiped Him in integrity of heart, He acted in a mighty way, astonishing everyone who heard the strange report. It was precisely the ark's seven-month captivity in Philistia that demonstrated God's supremacy — proving once again that faith is stranger than fiction.

A Jail That Couldn't Imprison

The apostle Paul knew all about God's taste for honoring true faith with unexpected surprises. He knew how the Lord loves to reverse the diabolical spin Satan tries to put on crucial events. Paul had learned that when evil mushrooms, it's time to look for some divine fungicide.

The little Book of Philippians illustrates what I mean. Paul's letter rings with praise and joy, just the right complement to a growing faith.

But at the moment Paul sat down to write his letter, untrained observers would have strained themselves to see any reason for such praise and joy and faith. The Romans had arrested Paul for preaching the gospel. Once the Apostle freely roamed the world, spreading the good news of Jesus Christ; now he found himself chained to a Roman soldier, prevented from spreading the Word of God.

Or was he?

It's true, a Roman guard sat next to him, chained to the

Apostle by cold iron. (Historians believe these no-nonsense guards relieved each other at regular intervals.) So in fact, Paul had lost the freedom to range far and wide in proclaiming the gospel.

But, dear reader, what do you suppose Paul would think of to discuss with Rome's finest? After hours of being chained to the dedicated evangelist, no doubt some soldiers began wondering just who was captive to whom! And in fact, that is apparently just what happened:

> Now I want you to know, brothers, that what has happened to me has really served to advance the gospel. As a result, it has become clear throughout the whole palace guard and to everyone else that I am in chains for Christ (Phil. 1:12–13).

Once again, in response to the faith of one of His children, God took a clear victory for the devil — the imprisonment of an effective evangelist — and turned it into a triumph of divine grace. What better way to evangelize tough Roman soldiers than to get down and dirty with them in close quarters over extended periods of time?

I think that would be enough to qualify as "stranger than fiction," but God wasn't done. Paul then said:

> Because of my chains, most of the brothers in the Lord have been encouraged to speak the word of God more courageously and fearlessly (Phil. 1:14).

Notice — it is *because* of Paul's chains that the Word of God went out boldly! I doubt that's what Satan had in mind when he had Paul tossed into prison. Yet that is just the sort of strange turnabout God loves to spring on His faithful people!

My, what a headache Satan created for himself! Not only did his attack make a way for the hard hearts of rough Roman soldiers to be softened by the gospel of grace, but it enabled God to create scores of evangelists where once there had been just poor, lonely Paul!

And it gets even stranger than that. In chapter 4 of his letter, Paul tells his Philippian friends that "All the saints send you greetings, especially those who belong to Caesar's household" (Phil. 4:22).

Imagine that! Satan, acting through Caesar, has Paul thrown into prison for preaching the gospel, confident that strong Roman chains would keep the message of Christ locked up. Instead, God sends His redemption message not only to grizzled soldiers who otherwise might never have heard it, but into the very home of Caesar himself!

Now, what writer of fiction could conjure up *that* kind of strange scenario? And who would believe it, even if he did? And yet that's exactly what God accomplished, in response to the faith of His dear children.

Anyone planning to oppose the King of the universe should take note: When you're dealing with the God of surprises, you can't be too careful.

Questions for further study

1. Read Romans 8:28.
   - A. Does Paul "guess" or "wish" that all things work for the good of God's children? Why is his word choice here important? How can he be so certain?
   - B. In how many things does God work for the good of His people? Does this always "feel" like the truth? Why or why not?
   - C. Note how Paul describes the people who can consider this verse a promise. In what two ways does he describe them? What is significant about both these descriptions?

2. Read Philippians 1:12–28.
   - A. What two unexpected blessings came from Paul's imprisonment (verses 12–13)? How do these amount to a weaving of extremes?
   - B. Verses 15–18 further describe the kind of reversal Paul mentioned in verses 12 and 13. What details do you learn here?

C. How did Paul regard his future (verse 19)? How is this a good example for us?

D. How are Paul's words in verses 20 through 28 a good illustration of what he wrote about in Romans 8:28?

E. In what way do verses 27 and 28 provide a fitting conclusion for Paul's remarks about his imprisonment? How do they teach us a biblical way to hope for a divine weaving of extremes?

3. Read Ephesians 3:20–21.

A. Who is the focus on in this passage? Why is this important?

B. What does this verse teach us to expect? How does it encourage you in your present circumstances? How does it relate to God's weaving of extremes?

ב

A Little Goes a Long Way

Sometimes we make the mistake of believing that God loves to honor only "super" faith, the kind of faith that only the "specially anointed" possess. We grow discouraged because we know we don't have such triumphant, mountainous faith — and we doubt whether we ever will.

Has such a thought ever troubled you? I confess, it has assaulted me. But remember, faith is stranger than fiction!

To be sure, God honors "great" faith. But He also knows great faith grows only from tiny seeds — say, mustard seeds. Tiny, maybe, but out of such miniature packages the Lord loves to grow enormous, shady bushes.

I probably can't ask for the best

I first met Floyd McClung about a decade ago, when a publisher contacted me about teaming with him to write a book for fathers. Floyd had worked for many years with a celebrated outreach organization called Youth With A Mission (better known as YWAM), and already had written the best-sellers *Living on the Devil's Doorstep* (about reaching men and women for Christ in Amsterdam) and *The Father Heart of God*. Now Floyd wanted to encourage fathers with some time-tested insights in *God's Man in the Family*.

As soon as I spoke with Floyd's lovely wife, Sally, and their two delightful children, Misha and Matthew, I knew he possessed the credentials to write such a book. In different ways, they all exuded a calm confidence born of a solid and loving relationship with Jesus Christ. When I first entered the world of the McClung family, Misha was in her early twenties and Matthew was nearing the end of his teens.

A few years after we finished the book, I started receiving newsletters from the family that asked for prayer regarding a strange, painful illness that had attacked Misha. Doctors seemed baffled to understand why nearly all the joints in her young body had begun to cause her great suffering. Even little movements sent stabbing pains throughout her limbs.

Eventually specialists began to unlock the mystery, but they could offer no medical help. At best they could recommend plenty of rest, a restricted diet, and long hours in a hot tub. After six torturous years, Misha learned from her doctors that she might never walk or travel again. Imagine what a blow this would be to any young person used to living abroad — and then consider that Misha had always longed to serve God on the mission field. But how can you do that if your body won't allow you to travel, let alone walk?

Floyd and Sally and hundreds of intercessors continued to pray for Misha, but she never received much more than occasional relief. Then one day a young man named Lionel Thompson came to visit. Floyd and Sally had known the Thompsons since before either couple had any children, but Lionel and Misha had never seen each other as adults. This first "adult" meeting left *quite* an impression, and Misha said to God, "That man is the best there is! But because I am sick, I probably can't ask for the best. . . ."

A statement of towering, overpowering faith? Probably not. But a mustard seed of faith? You bet.

As of June 1999, God still had not relieved Misha of her constant pain. Her physical condition had improved only a little, but in faith she left for an overseas mission trip with YWAM. That's when it happened. While working in Beirut, Lebanon, God totally healed her!

But that's only the first part of the story. It gets *better*.

Later that September, Lionel and Misha crossed paths in Colorado at a workshop with YWAM's University of the Nations. They thrilled to each other's company, and Lionel eagerly invited Misha to spend a week with him and his family members in Switzerland, where the Thompsons work with YWAM. Four weeks later Lionel and Misha teamed up again at a University of the Nations Leadership Training School in New Zealand, Lionel's homeland.

This means (if you haven't guessed by now) that Lionel and Misha dated and fell in love on three continents!

So it fits with the story that, at sunrise on February 8, 2000, Lionel proposed to Misha atop Auckland's Mangere Mountain. He had arranged for his love to be greeted and escorted up to the peak by painted Maori warriors, all of them holding torches in the dark to light her way. As this Christ-loving pair looked down over the city below, they were served communion together, then received prayers and blessings in both Maori and English.

Now there's one thing you should know about YWAM: it pays no salaries, but operates completely on faith. Therefore, staff members Lionel and Misha assumed they could never afford an engagement ring. It was enough that they and their families knew God had brought them together, and that this was His time for them to get engaged. Two days later, the newly engaged couple decided it would be all right, at least, to go and look at rings and dream toward the future.

They didn't know it, but a friend was praying for them at just that time. She perceived in faith that she was to call someone she had met only once. She knew only his name (Tony) and that he owned a surfboard shop. After trying three times, she finally located Tony and told him about her ringless friends.

"I don't even know why I'm calling you," she explained, "but maybe you would know a wholesale jeweler to help us find a ring?"

No, Tony didn't know of a wholesaler. But he did know something else. "Oh, I know exactly why you are calling me," he replied. "*I have your ring!*"

It turned out that, about the same time Misha was born, Tony's future father-in-law had bought a ring and proposed to a lady who declined his proposal. The man had kept the ring ever since; no finger had ever worn it. Once, Tony and his wife, Loran, tried to sell the ring, to no avail. Shortly afterwards God seemed to be telling them that He intended the ring for just one person, and that they were to hold on to it until He told them who that person was.

Enter Lionel once again. Without telling Misha a thing, Lionel hurried to meet Tony and see the ring. He prayed that if this were the right one, it wouldn't need to be sized. Of course, it fit Misha's finger as if it had been crafted just for her.

So it was that, to her great shock, Lionel proposed to Misha a second time — and on this occasion slid the "miracle" ring on her finger as the happy couple peered out over Auckland from the Sky Tower restaurant overlooking the soft lights of the city. And in one ceremony in New Zealand on March 20 and another in Kansas City, Missouri, on April 22, Misha McClung became Mrs. Misha Thompson.

Not bad for "mustard seed" faith, eh?

no scorn in his smile

Many times we can be harder on ourselves (and on each other) than God ever thinks of being. We punish ourselves with thoughts of unworthiness when we don't receive a prompt answer to prayer, and a few other believers seem even more eager to tell us that God ignores our prayers because we don't have enough faith.

A few years ago I looked around at the weak and sorry state of the Church and sat down to write a stinging rebuke. I thought a scornful re-do of the old hymn, "Onward, Christian Soldiers!" might do the trick, and here's what I came up with:

lay down, feeble christians!

Lay down, feeble Christians! Lounging as to snore,
With the cross of Jesus far behind once more.
Christ, the friendly Buddy, leads us to the show;
Stretch out on the sofa, see all troubles go!

Lay down, feeble Christians! Lounging as to snore,
With the cross of Jesus far behind once more!

Like a bear in winter, sleeps the church of God;
Brothers, we are resting, pamp'ring our dear bod;
We are not in motion, all one yawn are we;
One in entertainment, one in levity!

Lay down, feeble Christians! Lounging as to snore,
With the cross of Jesus far behind once more!

Lives and souls may perish, sin and error reign,
But the church of Jesus prostrate will remain;
Gates of hell will never fear a church so pale;
We have Christ's own promise, but we'd rather fail.

Lay down, feeble Christians! Lounging as to snore,
With the cross of Jesus far behind once more!

Lay down then, ye people! Join our happy throng,
Blend with ours your snoring, In the drowsy song;
"Sorry!" "Oops!" and "Pardon!" unto Christ the King;
Such will be the only gifts that we will have to bring!

Lay down, feeble Christians! Lounging, as to snore;
With the cross of Jesus far behind once more!

I'm glad I never went any further with *The Feeble Christian Hall of Fame*, the book project I dreamed up. At best, such a book would have been long on cleverness and woefully short on love. It's easy to scorn what you dislike — and too often we mistakenly think our bad habits reflect God's holy character. Let me explain what I mean.

Who wouldn't want to have "great faith"? If you call yourself a Christian, how could you not desire to move mountains by your triumphant faith? How could you not want to crush the doubt in your mind and replace it with victorious, evil-stomping, overcoming faith?

But here's where I think we make a terrible error. Because we would really like to have such "great faith" — but find that we do not — we begin to scorn anything that deviates from our idea of what such faith might be. Is someone suffering? Must be a lack of faith. Has a prayer gone unanswered for a long time? No doubt it's faithlessness. Does someone worry that a persistent pain might be cancer? Then he or she's an obvious candidate for the Feeble Christian Hall of Fame.

How is it that we forget God describes our Lord in the gentlest of terms? Remember? He says that Jesus "will not quarrel or cry out; no one will hear his voice in the streets. A bruised reed he will not break, and a smoldering wick he will not snuff out" (Matt. 12:19–20). Our loving Father insists that Jesus does not despise our weakness. He wants us to be strong, but He knows we'll never get that way through scorn.

Of course, God has every right to scorn our pitiful forays into faith. When we doubt Him, we doubt the omnipotent One, the Creator of the heavens and the earth, the absolute ruler of all that is. He has every right to scorn us.

But He doesn't, and He never will.

We can rest in the assurance that while our loving God will certainly exhort us, encourage us, even rebuke us when necessary, you'll never find Him scorning your genuine attempts at faith — no matter how little they may seem to you or to others.

A man of faith

Philip Peterson was born into the tender home of Dr. George and Lois Peterson more than half a century ago. He grew up in Beloit, Wisconsin, and I remember seeing his smiling face on many Sunday mornings at the People's Church, where my family and I attended. I never had a decent conversation with Philip, however. In fact, I never had one at all.

You see, Philip's severe mental disability had robbed his tongue of speech.

I'm sure Philip had to endure some teasing as he grew up, and I'm equally certain that Dr. and Mrs. Peterson spent long nights agonizing over their son. But when Philip died a few years ago, his mother remembered little of that. Mostly, she remembered his faith.

What's that, you say? That a young man with little capacity to think couldn't possibly have much faith?

Well, I don't know about that. But it certainly seems to me that he had at least a mustard seed worth of the stuff. After he died, his mother took the time to write down "Some of the things that Philip taught me." I think you might find her list surprising. She learned:

That life isn't fair — to anyone.
That self-pity can be an incapacitating disease.
That God is better at directing my life than I am.

That there are more caring people in the world than I know.

That being mentally retarded is an inadequate description
of a person.

That I am not perfect either, just human.

That asking for help and support is not a sign of
weakness.

That every child is truly a gift of God.

That joy and pain can be equally deep.

That you can never lose when you love.

That every crisis contains opportunity for growth.

That sometimes the victory is in trying rather than
succeeding.

That each person has a special purpose in life.

That I need to worry less and praise more.

That love can be measured in very small ways.

That the trust of a child is a treasure.

That the fruit of the Spirit (Gal. 5:22–23) can be
demonstrated without any verbal expression.

That God does not require us to understand our
circumstances, but only to trust Him completely.

That asking God "Why" is unacceptable.

That the meaning of salvation is beautifully simple and
understandable.

That God answers prayer in unexpected and unusual ways
and circumstances.

That the promises in Isaiah 43:1–3 are inexpressibly
precious.

— Lois Peterson, May 22, 1994

After reading that list, do you think God scorned Philip's little mustard seed of faith? Do you think our Father really couldn't hear Philip's words of faith just because he couldn't pronounce them?

Or do you think, as I do, that God treasures all of our genuine efforts at faith, regardless of how "simple" or "imperfect" or even "retarded" they might seem to others (or even to ourselves)?

Faith is stranger than fiction, I tell you — even when it comes to the amount that God requires.

And now I think it's time to cap off this chapter by hearing those "inexpressibly precious" promises that so encourage Lois Peterson, Philip's mom:

> But now, this is what the LORD says — he who created you, O Jacob, he who formed you, O Israel: "Fear not, for I have redeemed you; I have summoned you by name; you are mine. When you pass through the waters, I will be with you; and when you pass through the rivers, they will not sweep over you. When you walk through the fire, you will not be burned; the flames will not set you ablaze. For I am the LORD, your God, the Holy One of Israel, your Savior" (Isa. 43:1–3).

insight from the Bible

How much faith does it take to move the hand of God?

Our affluent age tends to "super-size" everything, from burgers to shopping malls. Mega-proportions have quickly become the norm. Bigger is not only better; now it's required.

But is it required in matters of faith?

Many earnest Christians would answer, "Yes!" They would insist, "The kind of faith God honors must be mega-sized. It has to dwarf the puny expectations of the common believer." They might even tell someone whose prayer seems to go unanswered that he or she just doesn't have enough faith. If only he or she could grow "great" faith, they say, then God would move in power.

Not so fast, the Bible says.

Only one person in Scripture is said to have "mega" faith, and that person was a desperate Canaanite, a pagan woman who implored Jesus to heal her demon-possessed daughter. After she kept after Jesus to grant her request, the Lord finally said to her, "Woman, you have great [*megale*] faith! Your request is granted" (Matt. 15:28). And from that hour, the woman's daughter was healed.

So great faith certainly *is* a great thing. But does that mean the rest of us are left out in the cold? If we haven't yet grown "mega" faith, can we expect no help from heaven? Do we have to lay up millions in faith deposits before we can make even the tiniest withdrawal?

Not according to Scripture. And that's another happy reason why faith is stranger than fiction.

"Little" versus "None at All"

Matthew 17 describes the awesome events that took place on the "Mount of Transfiguration," where Jesus, draped in blinding, heavenly light, appeared before Peter, James, and John. As the four descended from their glorious mountaintop experience, however, they ran headlong into a dark spiritual fog.

While the Lord and His top three disciples enjoyed a preview of heaven, the nine other disciples confronted the power of hell — and not so successfully, either. A distraught father had brought his demon-possessed son to Jesus' followers, in hopes that they could heal him. They failed. Jesus promptly cured the boy, but the nine wanted to know, "Why couldn't we drive it out?" The Lord replied, "Because you have so little faith," and then added, "I tell you the truth, if you have faith as small as a mustard seed, you can say to this mountain, 'Move from here to there' and it will move. Nothing will be impossible for you" (Matt. 17:19–20).

I'll admit that, at first, it appears as though Jesus rebukes His men for not having "great" faith. But a closer look at the passage dispels that notion. As New Testament scholar D.A. Carson explains, the word translated "little faith" (*oligopistia*) does not mean small in extent, but poor in quality. In Carson's words, "Jesus tells his disciples that what they need is not great faith (tiny faith will do), but true faith — faith that, out of a deep, personal trust, expects God to work."[1]

We know that's exactly what Jesus means, for the illustration He uses to picture God-moving faith casts the tiniest of shadows. Our Lord doesn't say we need mountain-sized faith, or ocean-sized faith, or even oak tree-sized faith. All He asks for is mustard seed faith. Faith doesn't have to start out big — it just has to be genuine. "The mustard seed is proverbially small, a suitable metaphor for the amount of faith needed to do the seemingly impossible," writes Walter Liefeld, another able New Testament scholar.[2]

In other words, *authenticity* is more important than *size* when it comes to faith. So it makes perfect sense that, time after time in the Gospels, Jesus isn't so amazed at the smallness of His followers' faith as He is at its total absence.

- "Why are you so afraid? Do you still have no faith?" He asked His disciples after quieting a storm they thought would kill them (Mark 4:40).

- "And he did not do many miracles there because of their lack of faith," says Matthew 13:58 of the unbelief Jesus encountered in His hometown, Nazareth.

- "He rebuked them for their lack of faith and their stubborn refusal to believe those who had seen him after he had risen," says Mark 16:14.

It is a wonderful thing to grow "great" faith. But now, as then, the Lord usually asks the same question of His followers: "Where is your faith?" (Luke 8:25). What continues to astonish Jesus is not our shrimp-sized faith (because He expects it to be whale-sized), but its disappearance altogether.

Fortunately for us, Christ has a second great surprise in store for those He loves: He doesn't abandon us because we fail, but rather works with us to move us to the next level.

one step at a Time

Mark's version of this "faith-as-a-mustard-seed" story contains a longer account of Jesus' interaction with the anguished father. When the Lord asks this man how long the demon had been troubling his son, he answers, "From childhood. It has often thrown him into fire or water to kill him. But if you can do anything, take pity on us and help us" (Mark 9:21–22).

If? Jesus seizes on that word "if" and replies, " 'If you can?' Everything is possible for him who believes" (Mark 9:24).

At that, the man breaks down. He knows he possesses nothing like mountain-sized faith. He can't even summon up boulder-sized faith. He might have great fear, but he doesn't have great faith. So in a faltering voice wavering with emotion, he immediately exclaims, "I do believe; help me overcome my unbelief!" (Mark 9:25).

And how does Jesus respond? Not with a rebuke. Not with irritation. Not even with advice on how to increase puny faith. Instead He turns and says to the demon, "You deaf and mute spirit, I command you, come out of him and never enter him again." The spirit shrieks, convulses the boy and comes out, leaving the lad looking so much like a corpse that many think he's dead. But not so, for "Jesus took him by the hand and lifted him to his feet, and he stood up" (Mark 9:27).

Now, what kind of faith did Jesus honor in this incident? Mountain-sized faith? Ocean-sized faith? Oak tree-sized faith? Or little, old mustard seed-sized faith?

Got any Grey Poupon?

The brilliant reformer John Calvin said of this believing-but-fearful man, "He declares that he *believes* and yet acknowledges himself to have *unbelief*. These two statements may appear to contradict each other, but there is none of us who does not experience both of them in himself."[3]

Isn't that the truth!

Of course, Jesus would love for us to develop great faith, but none of us starts out there. He does not despise our mustard seed faith, but rather honors it — to our benefit and His glory. And like any seed, when it's planted in good soil, gets plenty of water, and lots of sun, it grows. Growth is the name of the game in God's kingdom, and as the divine gardener, our Lord knows just how to coax little seeds into towering, ten-foot-tall mustard plants.

But such faith has to start somewhere.

By the way, don't make the mistake of thinking that we need genuine faith only to cast out demons or throw mountains into the sea. Our Lord made it clear that we need authentic faith even to get along with each other.

One day He told His disciples that they needed to forgive an offending "brother" as often as that individual repented of his offense, even if he did the same noxious thing seven times in one day. This sounded like substantially more than the disciples could handle, so they shouted out (wisely, I think), "Increase our faith!" (Luke 17:5). Jesus replied with a slight variation to the counsel He gave in the previous incident. "If you have faith as small as a mustard seed," He said, "you can say to this mulberry tree, 'Be uprooted and planted in the sea,' and it will obey you" (Luke 17:6).

Again — it's not the *amount* of faith that gives us problems; it's whether we have any *at all*. Jesus appears to be saying that if we truly understand the staggering amount that God has forgiven us, and if we truly have come to Him in faith and repentance, we don't really need "great faith" to forgive others. We can squeeze enough drops of forgiveness out of a single, tiny mustard seed of faith to cover oceans of offenses.

Why is that? Because faith is stranger than fiction. (And a lot more effective, too, as the Early Church found out one strange evening.)

It Must Be His Angel

What kind of faith does God love to honor? Does it have to grow to enormous proportions before He acts? Or does it simply have to truly *exist*?

We can get a big clue by investigating a late-night prayer meeting held in the early church.

Herod Agrippa I, the grandson of Herod the Great, decided he needed to boost his approval ratings. In an effort to gain favor among the people, he arrested several members of the Early Church. He executed James, the brother of John, and when his polling numbers rose, he jailed Peter during the Feast of Unleavened Bread.

The wicked king didn't want this high-profile prisoner to escape, so he threw Peter into a high security prison, chained him to two guards, and entrusted him to four squads of four soldiers apiece. Herod intended to try Peter after the Passover.

Things looked bad for the church. Really bad.

In faith the frightened church responded, calling together a late-night prayer meeting on Peter's behalf. We can only guess about what they prayed. That Peter would stand up for the faith? That Herod would change his mind? That Peter would be acquitted? That he would die as a faithful martyr? We just don't know, for the Bible doesn't tell us. It simply says, "The church was earnestly praying to God for him" (Acts 12:5).

Whatever the church requested, it turned out that God had bigger plans for Peter. In response to the faith of His praying people, the Lord sent an angel to the prison, freed the Apostle from his chains, and led him safely out of jail and back to freedom. At first Peter thought he was seeing another vision (as in Acts 10), but eventually he "came to himself and said, 'Now I know without a doubt that the Lord sent his angel and rescued me from Herod's clutches and from everything the Jewish people were anticipating'" (Acts 12:11).

The elated Apostle expected that the church might have come together to pray for him, so he hightailed it to the house of Mary, the mother of John, where in fact "many people had gathered and were praying" (Acts 12:12). But when he knocked at the outer door and called out to be let in, a servant girl named Rhoda recognized his voice and ran back to tell the others — without letting poor Peter inside. When she told the church, "Peter is at the door!" God's people replied with something less than mountain-sized faith.

"You're out of your mind," they told her.

When Rhoda kept insisting that she had made no mistake, God's praying people changed their minds and said — again, with something less than boulder-sized faith — "It must be his angel."

After all, they must have thought, *how could it be the flesh-and-blood Peter? That man is in prison, in a maximum security cell. No way he could be out.*

Yet what was that irritating knocking?

When someone finally opened the door, the church saw Rhoda had been right all along. It really *was* the flesh-and-blood Peter — and Luke says they were "astonished" (Acts 12:16).

Now, does that sound like mountain-sized faith to you? Boulder-sized? Oak tree?

Strange as it might seem, God had moved in power in response to the (mustard seed-size) faith of His believing children.

Shortly after this remarkable event, one of God's angels made a second appearance in the area. While an angel had awakened Peter in prison by striking him on the side, this time an angel struck again, but not for deliverance. This time the angel struck an arrogant King Herod so that "he was eaten by worms and died" (Acts 12:23).

And the church? "But the word of God continued to increase and spread" (Acts 12:24).

In other words, that mustard seed really began to grow.

Growing in faith

God makes it clear in His Word that He doesn't require mountains of faith before He will move in power on behalf of His dearly loved children. Yet at the same time, He tells us that He wants our faith in Him to increase. He wants our trust to mature. Seeds, after all — even little ones — are meant to germinate, blossom, and grow.

With that in mind, God describes for us in Scripture a number of strategies designed to help us grow in faith. While I have space to mention only a few of them, I encourage you to investigate each one (and put each one into practice!) on your own:

- *Obedience*. Passages such as Luke 17:3–10 and John 15:1–17 suggest that as we exercise our faith in obedience to God, the Lord will strengthen and increase our faith.

- *Study*. Acts 16:4–5 and Hebrews 5:11–6:3 imply that a reverent study of God's Word (when combined with obedience prompted by faith) leads to a deeper faith.

- *Service*. The apostle Paul tells deacons in 1 Timothy 3:13 that their faithful service will bring "great assurance in their faith." The same principle is certainly true throughout the Christian life.

- *Prayer*. Here I'm thinking not only of personal prayer, but of enlisting a prayer warrior on your behalf. The Thessalonians had such a person in the apostle Paul, who told them, "Night and day we pray most earnestly that we may see you again and supply what is lacking in your faith" (1 Thess. 3:10).

- *Hardships*. This might seem like a strange one, but the Bible insists that God intends hardships to strengthen our faith (2 Thess. 1:3–4; James 1:2–4; 1 Pet. 1:6–7).

- *Worship*. As we worship God for who He really is, we connect more and more with His power and glory. As this occurs, His holy will becomes increasingly clear, and we gain much power in prayer (Rom. 12:1–2).

As our desires increasingly mirror God's desires for us, our faith in Him grows. But we must guard against becoming arrogant or proud of the advances in faith we may enjoy. As in everything good, God is the ultimate source even of faith. The apostle Paul reminded us of this fact: "For by the grace given me I say to every one of you: Do not think of yourself more highly than you ought, but rather think of yourself with sober judgment, *in accordance with the measure of faith God has given you*" (Rom. 12:3, italics added). He emphasized this point again in 1 Corinthians 12:7–9, where he wrote, "Now to each one the manifestation of the Spirit is given for the common good. To one there is given through the Spirit the message of wisdom, to another the message of knowledge by the same Spirit, *to another faith* by the same Spirit" (italics added).

Thank God that the Lord responds to even the smallest expression of genuine faith — but thank Him even more that He nurtures that small faith so that it grows into something solid and substantial.

will He find faith?

In Luke 18:8 our Lord left us with one of the more gloomy questions recorded in the Gospels. After telling a parable intended to show the wisdom of persistent prayer, Jesus asked His disciples, "However, when the Son of Man comes, will he find faith on the earth?"

Now, why ask such a question?

I think He asked it because He could look far ahead into the future and see a time when "men will not put up with sound doctrine. Instead, to suit their own desires, they will gather around them a great number of teachers to say what their itching ears want to hear. They will turn their ears away from the truth and turn aside to myths" (2 Tim. 4:3–4).

I think He asked it because He knew "The Spirit clearly says that in later times some will abandon the faith and follow deceiving spirits and things taught by demons" (1 Tim. 4:1).

I think He asked it because He saw "There will be terrible times in the last days. People will be lovers of themselves, lovers of money, boastful, proud, abusive, disobedient to their parents, ungrateful, unholy, without love, unforgiving, slanderous, without self-control, brutal, not lovers of the good, treacherous, rash, conceited, lovers of pleasure rather than lovers of God — having a form of godliness but denying its power" (2 Tim. 3:1-5).

For good reason Jesus asked the question!

If you're still around when the Master returns, however, you can answer His question with a resounding, "Yes!" For despite whatever evil may be springing up around you, *you* can demonstrate faith — real, genuine, authentic faith. It may begin as small as a mustard seed, but if it's real, He likes it.

And count on this: no matter how small it may be, He'll find it when He returns!

questions for further study

1. Read Matthew 17:14–21.
   A. What was the problem described in this passage? Why could the disciples not deal with the problem effectively?
   B. What reason did Jesus give His disciples for their inability to resolve the problem successfully (verse 20)?
   C. According to Jesus, how much faith is required before God will move in power to answer our prayers? What is more important, the kind of faith or the amount? Explain.

2. Read Luke 17:3–6.
   A. Why do the disciples believe that they need greater faith to comply with Jesus' directions on forgiveness? What

is the connection between our faith and our forgiving those who injure us?

B. How much faith did Jesus say His disciples needed to be able to forgive someone who injured them? What is significant about this?

3. Read Romans 12:3 and 1 Corinthians 12:7–9.

A. In the Romans passage, why does Paul instruct his readers not to think more highly of themselves than they should? What does he mean by "measure of faith"? Who gave these readers this "measure of faith"?

B. In the Corinthian passage, how is the special gift of faith related to the other special gifts Paul mentions? Who decides which individuals get these special gifts? How is this significant?

3

Special Delivery

Until the last century or so, anyone who wanted a message or package delivered quickly to an address hundreds of miles away had to live with disappointment. It couldn't be done. People measured delivery times in weeks and months, not days or hours.

That began to change in the United States in April 1860 when the Pony Express, a system of mail delivery by continuous horse and rider relays, began operation between St. Joseph, Missouri, and Sacramento, California. The approximately 1,800-mile route, which ordinarily took weeks to travel, could now be covered in about ten days. Riders such as William "Buffalo Bill" Cody changed horses six to eight times between 157 stations. The completion of a transcontinental telegraph system in October 1861 doomed the immensely unprofitable Pony Express, but before it died it set an important precedent.

Within a few years the United States Postal Service developed a system for handling urgent mail. For almost a century only one such service existed: special delivery by the U.S. Postal Service. In 1979 several other companies entered the urgent mail business, but the term "special delivery" stuck. All of these systems recognize that some messages and projects can't wait for ordinary delivery; they need instant attention and extraordinary handling. Without special delivery, the message spoils and the project suffers.

Unfortunately, all human delivery systems eventually break down, as an old joke reminds me. A man heading for Los Angeles stands at the airline counter with his luggage. "Three bags to check, sir?" asks the counter attendant.

"Yes," replies the man, "and I'd like this one to go to Tokyo, that one to Rome, and the third sent to Buenos Aires."

"Sir, I'm sorry, but we can't do that," the employee apologizes.

"Why not?" the man demands, "that's what you did the last time I flew with you."

Human special delivery systems are like that — prone to break down, misfire, and threaten the projects dearest to our hearts. The good news is that God operates a Special Delivery system, too, and it always functions at 100 percent efficiency. His packages never get lost, never fall behind schedule, never become damaged in transport or spoil en route.

Even so, don't be fooled into thinking God's Special Delivery service operates without surprises. His packages always arrive on time — *His* time — but we never know when to expect them.

I should also probably mention that it's not so much *what* He delivers as *who*. For God's Special Delivery service is chartered to deliver His children from certain disaster; that's what makes it special.

You see, in God's urgent mail company, you're not only the package recipient, you're the package. It's *you* He delivers.

He Delivers Even to Uzbekistan

UPS won't deliver to some remote places. Federal Express can't reach every spot on the globe. Even special couriers can't venture into certain locales.

But God's Special Delivery service gets sidetracked by no red tape, intimidated by no geographical barrier, disheartened by no earthly difficulty. Our Lord delivers on time, every time — in His time. Even when the obstacles seem insurmountable.

A few years ago, Olga Avetisova supervised a ministry of mercy in the prisons, labor camps, and institutions of Uzbekistan (formerly part of the Soviet Union).

The warden of one of the prisons opposed Avetisova's ministry and refused to let her compassion workers inside. In response, the determined ministry director requested prayer from supporting congregations, asking that God would some-how open the way. They needed a Special Delivery if their work was to continue, so they dialed 1-800-SPECIAL DELIVERY. (Look for the Lord's advertisement in Psalm 50:15: "Call upon me in the day of trouble; I will deliver you, and you will honor me.")

God answered quickly and decisively, but not in a way anyone expected: A little while later the warden died in a plane crash. The new warden promptly opened the gates to the church workers.

"We didn't pray for her to die," Avetisova insisted, "but just that the door would be opened."[1]

No Delivery Too Small or Too Large

Dr. Ed Goodrick taught Bible and theology at Multnomah School of the Bible for many years. He fit the label of maverick if anyone ever did, yet those who knew him also insisted that no one loved the Savior more than he. That was always true, even in his early days as a young pastor in Mossyrock, Wash-ington.

Goodrick earnestly studied the Bible and preached it to the best of his ability. He worked hard at making the truths of Scripture come alive to his little congregation, and urged his parishioners to conform their lives to God's will. All his preach-ing and teaching centered on Scripture, which irritated several upper-class members of the church. They wanted someone a little more, well — *refined*. Someone who would teach the Bible less and discuss current events more.

Disgruntled parishioners urged church leaders to sched-ule a congregational meeting to review Goodrick's performance. Through the grapevine, the pastor heard that a sizable and in-fluential group within the church — led by the superintendent of the local school district — would call for his ouster. Goodrick loathed political maneuvering so he simply asked the elder board to judge him on whether his service met biblical standards. Then in simple faith he committed his situation to God in prayer.

By the time of the congregational meeting, Goodrick looked to be on his way out. On one side stood the superinten-dent and his party of high-powered supporters. On the other sat Goodrick and the church elders, most of whom made their living at logging and felt ill-at-ease with such politicking.

When the moment arrived for Goodrick's review, the chairman of the board, Neil Kjesbu, stood up. Kjesbu possessed none of the sophistication or erudition of the anti-Goodrick faction — he worked as a simple stump farmer and part-time mailman — but his character had earned him a powerful reputation in the community. People liked Kjesbu and they respected him . . . probably more than anyone else in Mossyrock.

So when Kjesbu rose, gave Goodrick a glowing review, and expressed the hope that their pastor would be around for a good, long time, the wind visibly rushed out of the superintendent's sails. Left almost speechless, he sputtered, "I don't know what you people think, but as far as I am concerned, if our pastor is good enough for Neal Kjesbu, he's good enough for me!" With that, he sat down and kept silent for the rest of the meeting.[2]

Moments later congregational members overwhelmingly asked Goodrick to stay on for another year, which ultimately turned into six. And God's Special Delivery service could add Pastor Ed Goodrick of Mossyrock to its long list of flabbergasted clients.

Recant or Die

On October 31, 1517, an obscure German monk named Martin Luther unintentionally touched off a religious firestorm that eventually incinerated Rome's absolute control of the Christian church. He gained fame for posting his 95 theses on the church door at Wittenberg as well as for his heroic speech before hostile delegates to the Diet of Worms in 1521.

But what is perhaps not so well known is the story of what happened to Luther immediately following his triumph at Worms. It demonstrates in classic style the truth that faith is stranger than fiction (Special Delivery subdivision). But to fully understand the reformer's awful peril, we have to back up a bit.

Luther never intended to start a new church, only to reform the old one. But in the years between his theses and the Diet of Worms, enormous differences of belief (and inflammatory statements on both sides) made that impossible. By the time state and religious leaders summoned Luther to appear at Worms to recant his beliefs and writings, he had endured several excommunications.

Aleander, one of the two Italian legates at Worms representing the pope, called Luther a "fool," a "dog," a "basilisk," and a "ribald," strongly urged the burning of his books, and threatened, "If ye Germans who pay least into the pope's treasury shake off his yoke, we shall take care that ye mutually kill yourselves, and wade in your own blood."[3]

Sounds like some church business meetings I've heard about. This was no pleasant walk in the park.

The emperor Charles, torn between political and religious interests, summoned Luther to Worms but did not know what to do with the reformer. If he handed him over to Rome, he risked armed rebellion in Germany. If he failed to repudiate Luther, he risked a dangerous falling out with the pope.

On April 2, 1521, Luther and three friends set out for Worms from Wittenberg, riding in a farmer's open wagon. He honestly hoped he would be allowed to defend his positions before receiving final judgment; but just before he left his hometown, the emperor ordered the reformer's books seized and forbade their sale. Luther would not find an unbiased tribunal waiting for him at the Diet.

Luther arrived in Worms on April 16 and was summoned before the Diet the next day. As he surveyed the impressive gathering of state and religious leaders, his confidence momentarily sagged. When asked to retract his books, Luther answered in a voice so low it could hardly be heard. He asked for more time to consider his response, "since it involved the salvation of the soul, and the truth of the word of God, which was higher than anything else in heaven or in earth."

The emperor granted him another day, and a gleeful Aleander reported to Rome that Luther entered laughing and left despondent.

On April 18 Luther again appeared before the Diet. This time, when asked whether he would recant his books, Luther answered with the famous words, "Unless I am refuted and convicted by testimonies of the Scriptures or by clear arguments (since I believe neither the pope nor the councils alone; it being evident that they have often erred and contradicted themselves), I am conquered by the Holy Scriptures quoted by me, and my conscience is bound in the word of God: I cannot and will not recant anything, since it is unsafe and dangerous to do anything against the conscience." Some historians doubt whether Luther actually spoke the following words, but they would be a fitting conclusion: "Here I stand. I cannot do otherwise. God help me! Amen."

Luther's public doubts concerning the church councils irked Charles, and the emperor finally decided to treat Luther as an obstinate and convicted heretic. Private negotiations between Luther and Charles failed to reconcile the two, and on April 25 Luther asked permission to return home — the most perilous trip of the reformer's life.

Luther and all his friends recognized the terrible danger. For although the emperor promised Luther safe conduct home, such assurances hadn't protected others. Just one hundred years before, a Czech reformer by the name of John Hus had been summoned to a similar Diet and was promised safe conduct by the emperor — but he had been seized, condemned, and burned at the stake.

In fact, Rome was planning to seize Luther just as it had Hus.

Shortly after the tribunal, Charles condemned Luther as "a devil in the dress of a monk." Philip Schaff, author of a majestic history of the Christian church, summarized Luther's predicament.

> Thus Luther was outlawed by Church and State, condemned by the pope, the emperor, the universities, cast out of human society, and left exposed to a violent death.[4]

On April 26 Luther began a slow trek back home. He stayed with friends and relatives on the way and preached often, although the emperor had forbidden him to do so. He knew his life hung by a thread, but he refused to flee as friends had advised.

At last the fateful day arrived.

On May 4 a band of armed horsemen suddenly rushed from the woods and surprised Luther and his group. In a chaos of cursing and swearing and utter confusion, the men seized Luther's carriage, yanked him out, forced him on horseback, and carried him away at full speed.

It all happened in broad daylight, but to Luther's companions it seemed as if night had fallen like a heavy curtain. It appeared as though Luther's worried friends had been right all along. His appointment with the stake could now be only hours away — and they could do nothing about it.

Luther and his abductors rode in silence until midnight, when the reformer learned he had been taken to the castle at Wartburg, where he would be detained as a prisoner of state in charge of Captain von Berlepsch.

But be careful about that word, "prisoner." When you're God's prisoner, as Luther was, you're apt to discover that faith really is stranger than fiction. In fact, God's angels had just made a remarkable Special Delivery.

Enemies from Rome hadn't seized Luther after all. Instead, men following the orders of the elector Frederick — Luther's friend and ruler of Saxony — had pulled off the kidnapping. Frederick (whom Aleander called "the fox") had secretly planned the whole thing in Worms.

Luther remained at Wartburg for almost 11 months, where under the assumed name of Junker Georg he translated the New Testament into German. For months Frederick kept his whereabouts secret. Even John, Frederick's own brother, didn't know where to find the reformer.

In one of the most pivotal events in church history, Frederick the Elector became God's means to keep Luther safe and to touch off what became the Protestant Reformation. The godly leaders of the Reformation resurrected and safeguarded the central doctrines of salvation by grace through faith alone and the sufficiency of Scripture alone as the Christian's rule of faith and practice.

It all happened through a divine Special Delivery. And so Martin Luther, too, learned that faith is stranger than fiction.

what's That in your Driveway?

I could recite several more stories of God's Special Delivery service, such as the one about the Christian evangelist in Saudi Arabia who was dragged into Islamic Court and accused of lying about supernatural healings connected with his ministry. Remember that a verdict of guilt in a Muslim court brings horrifying consequences. Into the courtroom marched 30 people suffering from various ailments. The prosecutor said, "If you are truly a man of God, then you will heal all of these people." Apparently that is just what happened, for sources say the evangelist was released and allowed to travel throughout the country without restrictions.[5]

Such stories thrill us, but I'd prefer not to continue recounting them. Why not? Because the real question is never, "Does God operate a Special Delivery service?" but "Do I believe He can deliver *me*?"

What do you say?

Of course, I can't predict what form God's deliverance might take in your case. Neither can I guess when He might knock at your door to make the delivery. He might appear tomorrow, He might wait for ten years. But I do know that He promises to deliver those who call on His name in faith. And I do know that when He acts in power, He often does so in some pretty strange ways.

So let me ask once again. Are you looking for God to deliver you? Are you convinced that He keeps His word? Are you willing to stake your life on the hope that He always answers His 1-800-SPECIAL DELIVERY line?

If you're in trouble, call Him. Expect Him to deliver. And give Him the glory when the heavenly mailman arrives. Say — could that be a delivery van I see pulling up into your driveway?

Insights from the Bible

God must love the delivery business, for no fewer than 203 times the Scriptures use some form of the word "deliver." The vast majority of these passages describe some sort of divine Special Delivery.

To my mind, however, the one Special Delivery that eclipses all the others — and the one that makes possible all the others — is the resurrection of Jesus Christ from the dead. In this most spectacular of all Special Deliveries, God delivered Jesus from death and the hand of Satan, just when the devil thought he had won it all.

A Long contest

Satan, of course, knew all about the prophecies of a coming Messiah who would save God's people from their sin. He also knew that this One would ultimately destroy *him* — unless He could be stopped. So from the very beginning the devil tried to derail God's promises of a divine deliverer.

One of his first schemes involved Abraham, the man through whom God promised to bless the whole world (Gen. 12–18). God said He would fulfill the promise through Abraham's *descendants*, even though Abraham was already an old man. Worse yet, Abraham's wife, Sarah, was barren. The text does not say so, but could it be that Satan first tried to defeat the promise by withering Sarah's womb? No son, no descendants. No descendants, no Messiah. No Messiah, no threat to Satan.

But our enemy likes "sure things." To hedge his bets, Lucifer incited Sarah to get Abraham to sleep with her maidservant Hagar, and so to "build a family through her" (Gen. 16:2). By this ploy the devil hoped to short-circuit God's promise. But this had never been God's plan and God did not honor the arrangement.

In the end, neither strategy worked. Almost 25 years after God first gave the promise — and with Abraham "as good as dead," according to the apostle Paul (Rom. 4:19) — God saw to it that Sarah bore a son. With the miraculous birth of Isaac, Satan's early assaults failed and God's Special Delivery operation retained its perfect record.

Hundreds of years later, the devil tried again, this time with more violence. Exodus 1 tells how Pharaoh grew alarmed over the multiplying numbers of Jews in Egypt and how he ordered all Jewish baby boys to be killed. Again — no descendants, no Messiah. But God averted the genocide and His good promise marched on.

During the time of the kings of Judah, Satan honed his tactics but kept to the same murderous strategy. (Murder always ranks among his favorite tools.) Except for the courage of one godly woman named Jehosheba, the royal line through whom the Messiah was to come (2 Sam. 7) would have perished:

> When Athaliah the mother of Ahaziah saw that her son was dead, she proceeded to destroy the whole royal family. But Jehosheba, the daughter of King Jehoram and sister of Ahaziah, took Joash son of Ahaziah and stole him away from among the royal princes, who were about to be murdered. She put him and his nurse in a bedroom to hide him from Athaliah; so he was not killed. He remained hidden with his nurse at the temple of the LORD for six years while Athaliah ruled the land (2 Kings 11:1–3).

Once again, God thwarted Satan's attempts to derail the promise of a coming Savior. The devil would make many more such attempts, but each time God confounded him.

Finally, the time came for Jesus the Messiah to step onto the world stage. By now Satan must have grown frantic. Even though his tactics had failed miserably through the centuries, he tried them once more. The devil prompted King Herod to send soldiers to the birthplace of Jesus "to kill all the boys in Bethlehem and its vicinity who were two years old and under" (Matt. 2:16). But God knew these evil schemes, too, and so provided a way of escape — another Special Delivery. Once more Messiah was spared.

But that did not stop Satan. During the years of Jesus' earthly ministry, the devil often tried to destroy God's promise. If he could not prevent Messiah from being born, at least he could try to defeat the Son's divine mission. Several times he tried to kill Jesus before the time set by the Father (Matt. 12:14; Mark 3:6, 11:18; Luke 19:47; John 5:18, 7:25; etc.). Each time he failed, sometimes in remarkable ways:

> All the people in the synagogue were furious when they heard this. They got up, drove him [Jesus]

out of the town, and took him to the brow of the hill on which the town was built, in order to throw him down the cliff. But he walked right through the crowd and went on his way (Luke 4:28–30).

Satan could not touch Jesus — until the time set by the Father. Finally, that time came. After years of plotting against Jesus, the Pharisees, Herodians, Sadducees, and others saw their chance. With demonic hosts fueling their hatred, they arrested Jesus, tortured Him, condemned Him to death, and convinced the Romans to crucify Him. It all happened so quickly.

Satan must have rejoiced (if that is possible) over what appeared to be his final victory. What he had sought to do for thousands of years at last he had accomplished. As Jesus coughed up blood and took his last few ragged breaths upon the cross, Satan must have thought he'd won. At last!

no sominex for satan

Still, I'd bet Lucifer slept poorly that night. Hadn't he seen Jesus raise Lazarus from the dead? Doubts must have nagged at him that, somehow, that awful death-conquering scene would replay itself in infinitely greater dimension.

Was he waiting for the "other shoe" to drop? Whether yes or no, early on Sunday morning, it did. And when it did, it crushed his head (Gen. 3:15). Resurrection Sunday showcased not only the most spectacular event in history — demonstrating for all time that faith truly is stranger than fiction — it also pointed up the most colossal misjudgment in all eternity.

The truth was, Jesus had *not* been caught up in a storm of events beyond His control. Far from it! Nothing happened which had not been planned from before the foundation of the world. Peter clarified these events in a famous prayer, while John supplied the timing:

Indeed Herod and Pontius Pilate met together with the Gentiles and the people of Israel in this city to conspire against your holy servant Jesus, whom you anointed. They did what your power and will had decided beforehand should happen (Acts 4:27–28).

. . . the Lamb [Jesus] that was slain from the creation of the world (Rev. 13:8).

Jesus died, not because of some overpowering satanic plot, but because God had chosen that unexpected means to win our salvation. Jesus died for our sins and rose again for our justification (Rom. 4:25). But not only that! For it was the devil's greatest "victory" that ensured his final destruction. The writer of Hebrews says it like this:

Since the children have flesh and blood, he [Jesus] too shared in their humanity so that by his death he might destroy him who holds the power of death — that is, the devil — and free those who all their lives were held in slavery by their fear of death (Heb. 2:14–15).

What the devil had schemed and labored to accomplish throughout human history, the Lord at last allowed him to achieve — to hell's everlasting ruin. When Jesus rose from the grave three days after His crucifixion, He sealed the evil one's doom forever. That is why the apostle Paul could write:

"Where, O death, is your victory? Where, O death, is your sting?" The sting of death is sin, and the power of sin is the law. But thanks be to God! He gives us the victory through our Lord Jesus Christ (1 Cor. 15:55–57).

That, friends, amounts to a classic description of history's ultimate Special Delivery. Because Jesus turned Satan's greatest triumph into his worst defeat, we too can expect victory when we place our faith in Christ. No matter how dark the skies may grow, no matter how desperate our circumstances may become, the resurrection of Christ — God's ultimate Special Delivery — teaches us to hold on tight to hope.

This is why you and I can move into arenas of human pain and expect to see God work. This is why we do not have to despair when disaster seems to threaten God's control of this world. As members of God's family bought by the blood of Christ, we are the sons and daughters of an almighty Savior who brings good out of evil and victory out of defeat. The devil does not have the final say; he has already pulled the switch for his own electrocution.

By placing your faith in the risen Jesus, you, too, can stand on the side of the God who delights in turning evil into good. Through faith in Jesus Christ who died and rose again, you may know certain victory over whatever circumstances trouble and harass you.

You say your life is crumbling around you? That does not matter. You say that for years you have been working for the other side? That does not matter, either. For God has enabled you, through faith, to join in Jesus' victory — faith not only for salvation in heaven, but for help and deliverance in this fallen world.

Throughout its pages, the Bible shows us that God loves to rescue His people out of their troubles, often in unexpected and unusual ways. Whenever you begin to doubt that, remember the Resurrection! Remember the empty tomb! If God can take Satan's most devastating attack and reverse it 180 degrees, no situation can become so dark or hopeless that it outstrips His power.

Not even yours.

confident to the end

Everything you have read hangs on the certainty that faith is stranger than fiction. But is that your conviction? Do you rest in the assurance that, no matter how bad things may look, God is still in control? More than anything else, that is what I long for you to take away from this book. It is my deep desire that you come to rest in the same confidence that comforted and energized the apostle Paul:

> What, then, shall we say in response to this? If God is for us, who can be against us? He who did not spare his own Son, but gave him up for us all — how will he not also, along with him, graciously give us all things? (Rom. 8:31–32).

This is the sure hope that allows us to carry on in a hurting world. Because faith is stranger than fiction, we can raise our tired eyes and look for a beautiful sunrise to appear in the very place where darkness now reigns. Bank on it! Jesus did, and things turned out pretty well for Him.

He's Not on Welfare

What do you suppose Jesus thought about as He hung on the cross? We know He thought about the criminal hanging next to Him, for He promised the man a place in paradise. We know He thought about those who crucified Him, for He asked His Father to forgive them. We know He thought about His mother's future, for He instructed John to take care of her.

We also know He thought about Scripture, for He quoted it: "My God, my God, why have you forsaken me?" (Ps. 22:1). Just as He had done throughout His earthly life, Jesus turned to the Scriptures for strength and hope during His final moments.

We don't know whether any other psalms tumbled through His mind, but I'd be surprised if they didn't. One day I plan to ask the Lord what Scriptures sustained Him as He carried the weight of our sin on His sagging shoulders. It wouldn't startle me to hear that Psalm 50 greatly encouraged His heavy heart.

Psalm 50 startles a lot of people these days. It's all too easy in a culture like ours to forget just how great a distance yawns between God and ourselves. We get so impressed with our technological and scientific advancements that we lose sight of the awesome power and glory of God. We foolishly begin to feel there's really not so much difference between the Creator and the created. That's why a text such as Psalm 50 can so shake us.

Psalm 50 confronts us with a God so supreme, so invincible, so utterly unlike ourselves that with a mere word He summons both the earth and the heavens. It brings us face to face with an almighty Judge before whom a fire devours and a tempest rages. It pictures a God so self-sufficient that, were it possible, He sounds almost arrogant. Listen to this God speak:

I have no need of a bull from your stall or of goats from your pens, for every animal of the forest is mine, and the catttle on a thousand hills. I know every bird in the mountains, and the creatures of the field are mine. If I were hungry I would not tell you, for the world is mine, and all that is in it (Ps. 50:9–12).

As Jesus hung on the cross, this is the God He had in mind. "The LORD does whatever pleases him, in the heavens and on the earth, in the seas and all their depths" (Ps. 135:6). Psalm 50 not only pictures an unstoppable, juggernaut deity of infinite power and authority, but a Heavenly Father who delights in delivering His children from hair-raising trouble. After the Lord declares His title as King of the universe, He adds this line: "Call upon me in the day of trouble; I will deliver you, and you will honor me" (Ps. 50:15).

You might call Psalm 50:15 the 1-800 number of Heaven's Special Delivery Service. The call is free ("call upon Me"), it's for urgent packages ("in the day of trouble"), and is guaranteed ("I will deliver you"). A payment plan is even detailed: "and you will honor Me."

The great English preacher, Charles Haddon Spurgeon, once preached on this text:

> God and the praying man take shares. First, here is your share: "Call upon me in the day of trouble." Secondly, here is God's share: "I will deliver thee." Again, you take a share — for you shall be delivered. And then again it is the Lord's turn — "Thou shalt glorify me." Here is a compact, a covenant that God enters into with you who pray to Him, and whom He helps. He says, "You shall have the deliverance, but I must have the glory. . . ." Here is a delightful partnership: we obtain that which we so greatly need, and all that God getteth is the glory which is due unto His name.[6]

The kind of Special Delivery described in Psalm 50:15 warms our heart and fuels our hope. For there are times when the skies grow so dark and the enemy so menacing that, should God withhold His hand, we would surely perish. But thank God the Bible assures us that faith is stranger than fiction! Just as Jesus called upon His Father to deliver Him in His greatest hour of need, so can we.

call now!

God addresses His promise in Psalm 50:15 to all of His children. That includes you. The deal is simple: you're in trouble; you call out to Him; He delivers you; you give Him the glory. As Spurgeon said, it's a delightful partnership.

So call that number, and expect to see a heavenly delivery van pull up to your curb, the company's slogan etched in gold letters on the van's side: CALL UPON ME — I DELIVER.

Questions for further study

1. Read 2 Kings 6:8–23.
    A. Describe Elisha's predicament. Imagine his predicament was yours. How would you feel? Would you panic? Explain.
    B. In what way did Elisha need a "Special Delivery"? How did he get it? What was the result?
    C. In what way was this "Special Delivery" surprising? Why do you think so many of God's "Special Deliveries" come with a surprise?

2. Read 2 Kings 11:1–16.
    A. Describe the predicament faced by the Jewish royal family. Who did God use to deliver little Joash?
    B. What elements of divine deliverance do you see in this passage? How did God use human ingenuity to further His purposes? How does this passage illustrate how God often "partners" with His children to bring about deliverance?
    C. God certainly delivered Joash in this passage, but others also were delivered. Who else was delivered, from what, and how?

3. Read Acts 16:16–40.
    A. What predicament did Paul and Silas fall into as described in this passage? How did this come about?

B. How did God rescue Paul and Silas from their predicament? What supernatural means did He use? What "natural" means did He use?

C. What was the outcome of this "Special Delivery"? In what ways can it be an encouragement to us?

4

You May Just Be
Surprised

On a hot South Carolina day in June, a godly friend of mine stood by the side of the Interstate and fumed. What was supposed to be the start of a great vacation had just taken a frustrating turn. It was a Sunday morning, he and his family still had 16 miles to go before reaching the outskirts of Knoxville — and the water pump on his car upped and died. Just like that.

My friend pulled over to the side of the road as the sun blazed down mercilessly, sending the thermometer skyrocketing into the nineties. Worse yet, John had no idea what to do. He needed to get to Myrtle Beach, where his father waited to spend five glorious days deep-sea fishing with his only grandsons (John's boys), but the overheated car refused to budge.

John tinkered with the motor for 20 minutes, to no avail. Meanwhile, cars whizzed by, not a single one stopping to offer help. After walking in circles for ten minutes — he says both to work up the courage and to get down the pride — John tried to flag down a car.

He might have spared himself the effort. No one paid the least heed. Cars continued to roar past, never even slowing down.

"Here I was on my knees, as it were," John writes, "with a flag in my hand, standing like the Statue of Liberty, and they didn't stop. It was humiliating."

It was also maddening. While John stood there, steaming

on the side of the road and still unsure what to do, his nine-year-old son walked up to him and announced, "I think we need to pray."

John looked down and answered, "You're right." He put down his flag, and right there by his paralyzed car, John prayed with his young son.

That's when God moved decisively to honor the faith of a family in distress.

"When we opened our eyes," John said, "two vehicles had pulled over. One of them was a mechanic. He looked at the car, diagnosed the problem and said, 'You know everything is closed today. If you go into town, you'll have to wait till Monday. I could go get the part and fix it here on the road for you.' "

You can guess the choice my friend made. Four hours later, he and his family joyfully resumed their journey. God had demonstrated His faithfulness once more.[1]

I consider this an encouraging story about answered prayer, but it also provides a great example of who often expresses faith — and who sometimes lags behind. Because in this story it's the little boy who first exercises the kind of faith that moves the hand of God. And it's his father — John Piper, a well-known pastor and theologian with a worldwide writing ministry — who lagged behind. John writes of this incident, "God loves to teach 9 year olds (and 43 year-olds!) lessons in faith and prayer."

Does He ever!

not where you most expect it

Sometimes we convince ourselves that God responds in power only to those with "great" faith, to the heroes and superstars and internationally known TV celebrities who claim to possess a special kind of "anointed" faith. Somehow we accept the dreadful notion that God sits in heaven like a stern Olympic judge, watching our every move and scoring our faith as if it were some kind of summer gymnastics event. Those who earn a 9.5 or better get answers to their prayers; the others can expect nothing but a cold shower and a curt rebuke to train harder.

Maybe next time, kid.

But this is all wrong. God doesn't wait to answer our prayers until we score perfect 10s on the vault of faith; He delights to respond even to trembling trust, in order to strengthen our frail spiritual muscles. Certainly He prefers strong faith to weak faith, but He knows you don't build championship athletes by denying them food and drink. He builds our faith over time by demonstrating His faithfulness, time after time.

And in any event, those whom we think ought to possess the greatest faith, oftentimes don't. Multiple conversations over the years with "insiders" at large ministries convince me that many of those we deem "giants of faith" — even those who claim to be able to summon great miracles of healing or knowledge or judgment — know little about the genuine article. Let me show you what I mean.

Wouldn't you think that the men and women who spend their whole lives studying the Bible would be among those most likely to exercise great faith? After three, four, or even five decades of poring over God's Word, wouldn't you expect such scholars to wield powerhouse faith?

The truth is, however, that many of them don't even believe the basics of the gospel.

Don't get me wrong; I wholeheartedly support earnest scholarship and the kind of hard study that takes place in seminary and graduate school. I have benefited tremendously from studying under some of the most godly, learned academics in the evangelical world. But the Bible itself warns us that some men and women — even seminary professors and religious academicians — are "always learning but never able to acknowledge the truth" (2 Tim. 3:7).

That sad reality became apparent once again during a recent ABC television special hosted by Peter Jennings. "The Search for Jesus" purported to be an unbiased report on how contemporary scholars view "the historical Jesus" — that is, the Jesus who really lived in Palestine 2,000 years ago. It quickly revealed itself, however, to be a mouthpiece for the kind of liberal scholarship that rejects all things supernatural. A hefty percentage of the "experts" Jennings interviewed advocate the views of the "Jesus Seminar," a group whose members reject the historicity of all but a tiny portion of the Gospels.

Time after time Jennings asked Robert Funk, John Dominic Crossan, and Marcus Borg for their take on what Jesus

was "really" like. This liberal trio, all active members of the
Jesus Seminar, proudly rejects most of the cardinal doctrines
of the Christian faith. In their view, Jesus was basically a bright
Jewish peasant who loved the common people, opposed injus-
tice, made a few memorable statements, and was executed by a
ruthless Roman state — but who certainly never was born of a
virgin in Bethlehem; certainly never performed most (if any) of
the miracles attributed to Him; certainly never claimed to be
God; certainly never predicted His death and resurrection; certainly never bore the weight of our sin or became an atoning
sacrifice; certainly never rose from the dead; and certainly never
promised to return to judge the wicked and reward the faithful.

In other words, their "faith" leaves them with "a roving
sage who preached a life of possessionless wandering and full
acceptance of one's fellow human beings, no matter how dis-
reputable or marginal . . . a Jesus for the America of the third
millennium, a Jesus with little supernatural baggage but much
respect for cultural diversity . . . an inspirational but purely
human figure who might have intended something different from
the dogmatic — and in the view of many, oppressive — faith
that grew up in his name."[2]

As might be expected, Jennings's special provoked a good
deal of controversy. The website *Belief.net* set up a forum to
discuss the ABC broadcast and encouraged readers to send in
questions to the featured scholars. One viewer asked John
Dominic Crossan — co-chairman of the Jesus Seminar and an
emeritus professor of biblical studies at DePaul University —
if he considered himself a believing Christian. (On the program,
Crossan suggested that followers never buried Jesus in a tomb,
as the Gospels claim, but that soldiers probably dumped His
corpse into a common grave along with other nameless criminals — and there His body rotted.) Crossan responded cheerily
that he's written over a million words on the historic Jesus, and
that should indicate his standing in the faith — although he'd
really rather be known as a "beliving" Christian, pardon the
pun.

We live in a time when our colleges, universities, and semi-
naries teem with learned men and women who not only disbe-
lieve the historic Christian message, but who actively oppose it

and try, from the "inside," to reshape it into something more acceptable. Typical among these non-believing Bible scholars is Burton L. Mack, formerly professor of New Testament at the School of Theology at Claremont. Mack believes that the Gospel stories about Jesus' death and resurrection amount to pure fiction and that no one knows what really happened. He wants to destroy the old faith and replace it with something more amenable to his social views. He blames Christianity for scores of contemporary woes, from genocide against Native Americans to unjust wars overseas. "It's over," he has said. "We've had enough apocalypses. We've had enough martyrs. Christianity has had a two-thousand-year run, and it's over."

One of Mack's former colleagues, James M. Robinson, disagrees with Mack's particular reconstruction of the historical Jesus, but agrees that Christianity must be revised. "I think that Jesus was an important person, one of the most important people who ever lived," he said, adding, "It's sort of a pity that all that most of us know about Jesus is from the creeds, which we can't believe in."[3]

One of those creeds that such skeptics "can't believe in" is called The Apostles' Creed:

> I believe in God almighty
> And in Christ Jesus, His only Son, our Lord
> Who was born of the Holy Spirit and the Virgin Mary
> Who was crucified under Pontius Pilate and was buried
> And the third day rose from the dead.
> Who ascended into heaven
> And sits on the right hand of the Father
> Whence He comes to judge the living and the dead.
> And in the Holy Ghost,
> The holy church,
> The remission of sins,
> The resurrection of the flesh,
> The life everlasting.

To scholars like Robert Funk, Burton Mack, Marcus Borg, John Dominic Crossan, and James Robinson, the Apostles' Creed is little more than a religious fairy tale, an unfortunate accretion of spiritual nonsense covering up the barest wisp of historical truth. No doubt they would applaud the comments of a speaker at "Global Gathering III," a 1997 event sponsored by the United Methodist General Board of Global Ministries. Nancy Periera, a Brazilian theologian, urged 4,000 conference attendees to make no distinction between Jesus and the world's other children; she believes all should be reverenced as little messiahs. "The crucifixion of Jesus Christ revealed an abusive heavenly Father who is not fit for Christian worship," she also declared. "We have to stop praising Jesus' cross . . . We have to look at Jesus' cross as a tragedy, a human episode without any meaning."[4]

Do we *really*?

Friends, we live in a perverse, twisted age. We insist on our right to do what the Bible expressly condemns, yet we piously protest when we reap painful consequences. We don't want to be ill thought of, but we don't want to change our conduct, either. Mothers kill their babies, but don't want to be considered bad parents. Fathers come home plastered, but don't want to be called drunks. Tax cheaters file false returns, but dislike the label of liar. Drug abusers contract a fatal disease, then sue the city for failing to prevent them from acquiring needles. And professors of religion want to deny all the cardinal doctrines of the historic Christian faith, yet still be called believers.

In short, we want to be happy, healthy, well-respected little wretches.

It comes down to this: Despite what we might think, robust faith doesn't always grow best in the fields that receive the most fertilizer. Great learning does not necessarily translate into great faith; neither does great oratorical ability, great charisma, great popularity, great buzz, or great claims.

Maybe we'd all be surprised to learn whose faith God honors the most.

faith in unexpected places

Joshua Sundquist knew something just couldn't be right; healthy eight year olds shouldn't be bothered by consistent leg pain. Medical tests soon revealed he suffers from Ewing's Sarcoma, a fast-growing bone cancer, and before long doctors decided they had to amputate Joshua's left leg. Fifteen nauseating chemotherapy treatments followed.

Yet despite the trauma, young Joshua could confidently say, "God was with me through everything. I especially thought about several of my favorite verses. Joshua 1:9 says not to fear because we know that God is with us and He is Lord. This means that wherever we are, whatever we're doing and whenever it is, God will be with us. That's why we don't need to be afraid."[5]

Joshua might be young, but he exercises more genuine faith than many of us do. "I think that many times when someone is having a hard time," he says, "people just recite Romans 8:28 and say, 'See, God says that this major disaster in your life is good. So be happy. Bye.' That's just not the way it works. A lot of times bad things happen that just seem bad for the rest of our lives, and we don't know why God let them happen. But that doesn't mean those things can't help others or strengthen your own faith. They will always glorify God in the end, whether we see how or not."

But does such strong faith hold up for long under stress? In Joshua's case it has. Five years after he lost his leg, Joshua could still say, "God has blessed me very much. He has helped me to overcome and persevere through my problems. He will do the same for you if you trust him and remember that circumstances don't last forever. But God does."

Circumstances don't last forever. But God does.

Wow! Now, *that's* faith!

Adam Gustafson shared a similar kind of triumphant faith, if not a similar medical prognosis. Told that he suffered from an inoperable brain tumor, he refused to accept a verdict of death and chose to believe that God would heal him. He took to calling his tumor "Fred" and kept repeating the phrase, "Drop dead, Fred." Yet in his case, God did not choose to bring physical healing. Just months before his death on November 4, 1995, Adam told his dad, "I'm in a win-win situation. If God heals me I can ride my bike and I win. If God doesn't heal me, I go to heaven to be with him, and I still win."[6]

If that's not great faith, what is it?

I first learned of these tremendous stories of genuine faith through my friend Dave Dravecky. Baseball fans remember Dave as an all-star pitcher for the San Francisco Giants in the mid to late eighties. His career came to a sudden end in 1990 when cancer forced the amputation of his pitching arm. Ever since then he and his wife, Jan, have run "Dave Dravecky's Outreach of Hope," a ministry of compassion that reaches out to amputees and cancer victims.

I got to know Dave and Jan through several book projects we tackled together. They publish a tremendous newsletter called *The Encourager*, one edition of which focused on heaven.[7] I couldn't help but smile when I read how several of their young friends, whom they met through the work of the outreach, described the place where God lives.

"There are roads of gold, gates of pearl, and after you have walked through the gates of pearl, I think you might see a humongous throne," said seven-year-old Emily Edwards. "I think the throne is made out of bricks of gold and outlined with pearls, decorated with emeralds — maybe even rubies! I don't know if I'm right, but I do know you will have to have bare feet."

Three-year-old Micah Leake insisted that "The best part of heaven is the party Jesus is going to give us. Lots of babies will be in heaven. If we need our dolls in heaven, Jesus will have them there."

Another three year old, Jacob Knepper, didn't concern himself so much with dolls as with food: "I think heaven would have fences in it with strawberries. David who fighted Goliath would be there, too. I think heaven would have blueberries and gold in it. Old people will be there and God's angels. There also will be a big, big feast that keeps everybody full."

Jacob's older sister, Heather, proved that even 11 year olds can know for sure what heaven's all about: "Heaven will be the greatest place ever, but mainly because Jesus will be there. To get to this great place, though, you must believe in Christ our Lord."

And I'll leave it to Taylor Andrews, 13, to put the capstone on these delightful expressions of genuine faith. "God says that heaven is perfect for everyone, and we each have our own idea of what perfect is," he said. "My dad died, so part of my perfect heaven would be to have my dad there with me. Best of all, we could see God whenever we wanted."

Look no further for the kind of faith God loves to honor! It may not be sophisticated, but it's real. It may not win headlines, but it's genuine. It may not wow the crowds, but it's growing.

Whose faith do you think most delights God, the unshakable trust of a three year old who's looking forward to heavenly blueberries, or that of a popular TV personality-turned-author who hasn't had to trust God for anything since he or she made it to the best seller list? In a topsy-turvy world where faith is stranger than fiction, we often find genuine trust in God where we least expect it, and find it missing where we thought it had to be.

Let me leave you with an old story from an old book. *Token for Children* was written over a century ago to tell the moving tales of several real children who lived long ago. The book details their conversion, life, and triumphant deaths.

One such story concerns a seven year old named Jacob Bicks. When Jacob came down with a severe illness his parents wanted to send for the doctor, but their son knew he had moved beyond the help of earthly physicians. "No, the Lord will help me," he replied. "I know He will take me to himself, and then He will be all my help."

The dying boy's father could hardly believe the spiritual confidence of his young son and replied, "Oh, my dear child, you have such strong faith."

Jacob looked up feebly at his father and said, "Yes, God has given me such a strong faith in himself, through Jesus Christ, that the devil himself will flee from me." By then out of breath, the exhausted child grew silent for a moment, then spoke a final, short prayer: "Lord, be merciful to me, a poor sinner."

And then he leapt straight into the arms of Jesus.

Jacob died in Holland more than three and a half centuries ago, but his kind of strong faith lives on. It exhorts us to drive ahead in faith, no matter our circumstances, no matter how feeble or weak we might consider our faith to be.

As Jacob himself might say to us, with a grin, "You may just be surprised."

Insight from the Bible

When you're ready to build a house, to whom do you turn? A building professional.

When you need counsel about the law, to whom do you turn? A legal professional.

When you want to install a new telephone system, to whom do you turn? A communications professional.

So it would only make sense that when you're looking for genuine faith, you'd turn to a religious professional, right? Not necessarily.

That's one of the strange things about biblical faith. Sometimes, faith is stranger than fiction not only in who has it, but in who doesn't.

Amazing faith (and unbelief)

Although no fewer than 43 times the Gospels use some form of the word "astonished" or "amazed" to describe the stunned reactions Jesus provoked by what He said or did, only in two incidents are we told that something "amazed" or "astonished" our Lord. Both incidents involved faith — either who had it, or who didn't.

The first event, recorded in Mark 6, describes the time Jesus returned to His boyhood town of Nazareth. As He taught in the local synagogue, "Many who heard him were amazed" at His teaching and wondered aloud how the neighbor kid could have gained such knowledge. The more they talked among themselves, the more irritated they became at what they considered to be nothing but an impudent upstart. Mark says simply, "And they took offense at him" (Mark 6:3).

Jesus stared at the unbelief swelling around Him — a severe drought of faith where there should have been oceans of it — and said to the Nazarenes, "Only in his hometown, among his relatives and in his own house is a prophet without honor." Mark concludes his report with the sad words, "He could not do any miracles there, except lay his hands on a few sick people and heal them. *And he was amazed at their lack of faith*" (Mark 6:5-6, italics added).

Not many things amazed Jesus — it's tough to astonish

the Creator of the universe — but unbelief among those especially groomed for faith certainly did the trick. Somehow, where
faith should have grown strongest, it wilted altogether.

Strange.

Luke records a happier incident in the seventh chapter of
his Gospel. While visiting Capernaum, Jesus heard about the
dying servant of a Roman centurion. This Gentile army officer
wanted the Master to heal his servant, but he didn't feel worthy
of a house call. Before Jesus arrived at his door, the centurion
sent friends with an amazing message: "Lord, don't trouble yourself, for I do not deserve to have you come under my roof. That is
why I did not even consider myself worthy to come to you. But
say the word, and my servant will be healed. For I myself am a
man under authority, with soldiers under me. I tell this one, 'Go,'
and he goes; and that one, 'Come,' and he does it" (Luke 7:7–8).

For only the second time in His ministry, Jesus stood there,
astonished. Luke says, "When Jesus heard this, *he was amazed
at him*, and turning to the crowd following him, he said, "I tell
you, I have not found such great faith even in Israel" (Luke 7:9,
italics added).

Now remember, the Romans were the "bad guys" in Jewish
history — the barbarian conquerors, the Gentile dogs, the pagans, the idol-worshiping, pig-flesh eating, uncircumcised brutes.
And yet Jesus publicly announced that this particular Gentile
dog had greater faith than anyone in the whole of kosher Israel.

Strange.

Faith isn't always where you expect to find it, and it sometimes shows up where you'd never guess to look. That's one
reason why it really is stranger than fiction.

Models with unwrinkled faces

If you were asked to find a model for strong faith, where
would you look? Forget about specific individuals for a moment and think more in terms of classes or groups of people.
Where would you search for models of genuine faith? In semi-
naries? Church offices? Mission headquarters? Among celeb-
rity Bible teachers?

When Jesus looked for models of strong faith, He repeatedly turned to the same unexpected group: children.

At that time the disciples came to Jesus and asked, "Who is the greatest in the kingdom of heaven?" He called a little child and had him stand among them. And he said: "I tell you the truth, unless you change and become like little children, you will never enter the kingdom of heaven. Therefore, whoever humbles himself like this child is the greatest in the kingdom of heaven" (Matt. 18:1-4).

And again:

People were bringing little children to Jesus to have him touch them, but the disciples rebuked them. When Jesus saw this, he was indignant. He said to them, "Let the little children come to me, and do not hinder them, for the kingdom of God belongs to such as these. I tell you the truth, anyone who will not receive the kingdom of God like a little child will never enter it." And he took the children in his arms, put his hands on them and blessed them (Mark 10:13–16).

And again:

At that time Jesus, full of joy through the Holy Spirit, said, "I praise you, Father, Lord of heaven and earth, because you have hidden these things from the wise and learned, and revealed them to little children. Yes, Father, for this was your good pleasure" (Luke 10:21).

And yet again:

The blind and the lame came to him at the temple, and he healed them. But when the chief priests and the teachers of the law saw the wonderful things he did and the children shouting in the temple area, "Hosanna to the Son of David," they were indignant. "Do you hear what these children are saying?" they asked him. "Yes," replied Jesus, "have you never read, 'From the lips of children and infants you have ordained praise'?" (Matt. 21:14–16).

Time after time in the Gospels we find Jesus pointing to the faith of children as a good model for our own faith. And what is it about the faith of children that He wants us to emulate? It can't be that Jesus wants us to *think* like children. He certainly has no desire that we believe everything that nice people tell us. We know this because He never contradicts himself, and in 1 Corinthians 14:20 He inspired the apostle Paul to write, "Brothers, stop thinking like children. In regard to evil be infants, but in your thinking be adults." In a similar vein, He inspired the apostle John to write, "Dear friends, do not believe every spirit, but test the spirits to see whether they are from God, because many false prophets have gone out into the world" (1 John 4:1).

So what is it about the faith of children that our Lord wants us to build into our own, maturing faith? I think the preceding passages suggest two primary elements, one positive and one negative.

Positively, we are to mimic the *dependent receptivity* of children. Children *receive* the kingdom of God, they don't earn it or win it or try to qualify for it. They *depend upon* someone great to give them what they can never deserve. They come to Jesus palms up, trusting that He will fill their empty hands with good things.

That is the only way to build a strong, growing faith. Self-sufficient faith is a contradiction in terms. The only kind of faith that God honors is the kind that depends on Him to do for us what we can never do for ourselves. Genuine faith marvels at the goodness of God and increasingly learns to depend on Him and receive from Him whatever He deems best.

But I think there's something else about the faith of children that qualifies it to model the kind of trust God wants adults to develop. That is, it lacks something that many of us have (in spades).

The Issue Is Pride

For the most part, little children don't feel self-conscious. They don't constantly worry about what they wear or where they live or who might see them with whom. They simply take life as it comes, unconcerned about appearances or reputation or social standing. When they feel like laughing, they laugh.

When they feel like crying, they cry. And when they feel like praising, they praise.

That was precisely the issue in the passage from Matthew 21. The chief priests and teachers of the law — dignified, stately, and consumed with decorum — loathed the spontaneous praise offered to Jesus by the shouting, laughing children. These self-obsessed men insisted that Jesus rebuke the kids for their unseemly outburst.

But Jesus did a strange thing. Not only did He refuse to scold the children; not only did He approve of their behavior; but He publicly honored the kids for their faith, noting pointedly that they had just fulfilled sacred prophecy!

In so doing Jesus actually rebuked the chief priests and teachers of the law. Why? Because their self-absorption and pride prevented them from offering the kind of spontaneous praise at which kids excel. Christ's rebuke reminds us that faith and pride simply cannot co-exist.

That is why our Lord told His disciples, "Whoever *humbles himself* like this child is the greatest in the kingdom of heaven" (Matt. 18:4).

That is why Jesus reminded His followers, "Anyone who will not *receive* the kingdom of God like a little child will never enter it" (Mark 10:15).

That is why the Son could joyfully thank His Father for "hiding" the truth from "the wise and learned" and "revealing" it to "little children" (Luke 10:21).

In each case, the issue comes down to pride. Luke's version of the Mark 10 passage even begins with Jesus saying, "For everyone who exalts himself will be humbled, and he who humbles himself will be exalted" (Luke 18:14). Genuine faith never calls attention to itself or gets puffed up over how much it's grown.

The apostle Paul followed Jesus' lead in making this connection between lowliness and faith, pride and unbelief. He reminded the Corinthians:

> Brothers, think of what you were when you were
> called. Not many of you were wise by human stan-
> dards; not many were influential; not many were of

noble birth. But God chose the foolish things of the world to shame the wise; God chose the weak things of the world to shame the strong. He chose the lowly things of this world and the despised things — and the things that are not — to nullify the things that are, so that no one may boast before him. It is because of him that you are in Christ Jesus, who has become for us wisdom from God — that is, our righteousness, holiness and redemption. Therefore, as it is written: "Let him who boasts boast in the Lord" (1 Cor. 1:26–31).

Children might boast about their rich or strong daddy, but you'll never hear a kid bragging about his or her amazing ability to receive help from The Big Guy. It just wouldn't make sense. The other children would drop their baseball mitts and Barbie dolls and stare at the kid as if caterpillars were crawling out of his nose.

No one builds their faith by obsessing on their faith — any more than they build a home by obsessing on the lumber delivery trucks. The best way to build a house is to book a superior contractor, and the best way to build your faith is to spend time with God and His Book, searching out all the ways He proves to be a superior God.

A sobering warning

What does all this mean for us? For one thing, it means that if you ever meet a man or woman who brags about having "great faith," you know he or she has missed out on the real thing. And make no mistake, Jesus predicted that many professing believers would miss it badly:

> "Not everyone who says to me, 'Lord, Lord,' will enter the kingdom of heaven, but only he who does the will of my Father who is in heaven. Many will say to me on that day, 'Lord, Lord, did we not prophesy in your name, and in your name drive out demons and perform many miracles?' Then I will tell them plainly, 'I never knew you. Away from me, you evildoers!'" (Matt. 7:21–23).

After a statement like that, can there be any question that faith is stranger than fiction — particularly in who has faith and who doesn't? It seems natural to think that only great faith would enable a person to prophesy in Jesus' name, to drive out demons, to perform miracles (and not one or two, but "many"). Yet Jesus insisted that a host of faithless men and women will appear before His throne at the end of history to plead their cases. They will provide all kinds of compelling exhibits and testimony that seem to point to real faith — evidence that Jesus won't bother to discount. Apparently, they really will have done all those things.

The only thing Jesus will say is that He never knew them.

Looked like faith. Walked like faith. But smelled a lot like smoke, and you know where smoke belongs.

So don't be deceived by counterfeits. And don't believe the lie that "great" faith is reserved for the superstars, the celebrities, and the famous.

If you can learn from a child, you too can exercise great faith. And won't your Daddy be pleased?

questions for further study

1. Read Matthew 15:21–28.
   A. What is significant about the woman being a Canaanite?
   B. What request did the woman make of Jesus? How did He respond? Why did He respond like this?
   C. Why did Jesus finally tell the woman that she had "great" faith? What was "great" about it? How did Jesus respond to this "great faith"?
   D. What does this passage teach us about the nature of "great faith" and about who can possess such faith?

2. Read Luke 7:1–10.
   A. Describe the situation reported in this passage. What happened?
   B. List all the details this passage gives regarding the centurion.
   C. How did the centurion display his faith? Where do you suppose he got this faith? How could he express such

faith in Jesus, having never met the Lord?
   D. What does this passage teach us regarding who can exhibit "great" faith?

3. Read Matthew 18:1–4, Mark 10:13–16 and Luke 1:21.
   A. Who is described in these passages? What kind of faith do they have?
   B. What elements of this sort of faith are we to emulate? How can we do so?
   C. Do you ever struggle with expressing this sort of faith? Explain.

5

Screwups to the Glory of God

My senior year in high school I won the lead role for Beloit Memorial's production of *Flowers for Algernon*. I played Charlie Gordon, a pleasant but mildly retarded young man whose IQ rockets to well over 200 through an experimental surgery. At the height of his genius Charlie makes a horrible discovery: His increased intellect came only through irreversible injury to his brain. He learns that the more intelligent he becomes, the faster and further he will descend into confusion.

Toward the end of the play, Charlie sits alone in his spartan apartment when someone knocks at the door. He doesn't want any visitors. Although he has already begun his tragic decline, he still remembers his brilliance. He cannot stomach pity, so he orders his caller away — a profound scene in an emotionally wrenching drama.

As a captivated audience of several hundred watched, I prepared to shout my pitiful line. I was supposed to say, "I want to be alone!" Instead, the words *I want to be by myself!* flashed through my mind. And before I could do anything about it, I heard myself screaming, "I want to be by my alone!"

I blanched and the audience howled . . . but not, I found out later, because of my blunder. No one other than the cast knew I had mangled the line. Spectators thought it sounded perfectly appropriate; it illustrated Charlie's rapid deterioration, provided some much-needed comic relief, and in a strange way even highlighted the greater tragedy to come.

Saved! I screwed up, but in an unexpected way my bungling actually enhanced the performance.

mistakes + god + faith = surprises

Most of us can tell similar stories. Our mistakes, blunders, and assorted screwups somehow get transformed into blessings. Probability helps to explain much of this — the sheer number of our errors guarantees that one of them, somewhere, sometime, by blind chance is going to turn out well.

Christians, however, enjoy a much more lively hope. Those who are members of God's family through faith in Jesus Christ can rest in the certainty that God is an expert at taking their gaffes and using them for His glory. Our Heavenly Father delights in revealing His majesty through our mistakes.

This chapter was written to people who want to serve and obey God, but who fear their mistakes or (repented-of) sins disqualify them for further divine use. It was written to Christians who long to be holy, but who find "the spirit is willing but the flesh is weak." It was written to all those who mean to run with the godly but occasionally trip, fall, and skin their knees.

Remember this: God is never bound by our mistakes! Our very human blunders do not disqualify us from a useful role in God's reclamation project for this old earth. Those who earnestly desire to serve God — but who doubt they can find work shoes to fit their feet of clay — should read on.

A few years ago, for example, I was asked to speak at a banquet for a Crisis Pregnancy Center in Albany, Oregon. I have known for years about the invaluable work CPC does across our nation with hurting women, so I was delighted to accept the invitation. I asked a few perfunctory questions about who and how many might be attending, where and when the banquet was to be held, and whom to contact should I need further information. I didn't bother to make a few other inquiries that would have helped me prepare more effectively.

As I thought about an appropriate Bible text for the evening, I finally chose Galatians 6:9: "Let us not become weary in doing good, for at the proper time we will reap a harvest if we do not give up." It made perfect sense to me: people dedi-

cated to saving the lives of unborn children become obvious
targets in this culture for all kinds of abuse. I reasoned that if
anyone needed encouragement to keep on "doing good" it would
be the faithful workers at the Crisis Pregnancy Center. I could
hardly imagine what kind of attacks they had been forced to
weather over the years.

The night of the banquet, I left Portland early for the two-
hour drive to Albany. Although I have a tendency to get lost, I
found the right place easily, stopping just once to get my bear-
ings. I made my way to the banquet hall and soon was greeted
by Patty Mahockle, at that time the Albany CPC executive director. We chatted for a few moments when she casually dropped
the bombshell. "We're so glad to have you here this evening,
Mr. Halliday," she said. "We're hoping that this will be a fine
kickoff for the Albany CPC."

Kickoff? I wondered. *Could I have heard incorrectly?*

So I asked. "A kickoff — for your new fiscal year, you
mean?"

"I suppose you could call it that," she replied. "Actually,
this is our first annual banquet. We're hoping this will give us a
good foundation for many years of ministry."

Foundation, did she say? As in, *start?*

Now serious worry began to set in.

"Ummm, when did you actually open your doors to the
public?" I stammered.

"We hope to open our doors in a week or so," she replied,
smiling.

As my heart sank to my toes, I began to see my talk cough,
sputter, and die. How could it still be relevant? Even so, I managed a weak, "Ahhh — so let's see, then. You, uhh, haven't
opened for business yet?"

"No, that's right," she acknowledged. "But we're really
excited about getting underway. Mr. Halliday, could you excuse
me for a moment? I have to see to some details before we get
started tonight. We're looking forward to your talk!"

As Patty left, I berated myself for not asking a few obvious questions. I had just assumed the center had been open for
some time. It never occurred to me that this banquet would
serve as its coming-out party.

But now I was stuck. With no time to change topics or Scripture passages, I breathed a short prayer that God would use my remarks. I convinced myself that even if no one in the audience needed such a talk right now, they would in a few months. Slight consolation, but it allowed me to go on.

When I gave my talk, it appeared, at least, that I held the audience's attention. I hoped that even though my speech missed Albany's needs, someone in the crowd would be encouraged by it. God's Word never returns to Him void, after all . . . even when it's delivered by a less-than-prepared servant.

What happened next reminded me that faith really *is* stranger than fiction.

The chairman of the CPC board approached me and asked if I had been told about his organization's history. *Oh boy,* I thought, *here it comes.*

"No," I said, "I can't say that I have."

"Well, that's interesting," he replied, "because your message hit the mark exactly."

Say what?

"What do you mean?" I asked, more in shock than curiosity.

"About a month ago we discovered that $5,000 had been misappropriated from our account," he replied. "And you know that these centers are run on a shoestring. It nearly did us in — we almost quit before we began.

"And then, just yesterday, we found out that our rent is going to be 50 percent higher than we had planned for. That was almost the straw that broke the camel's back. Many of us came to this banquet discouraged, really down. Your talk was just what we needed to hear. Thank you!"

The man vigorously pumped my hand while exclaiming, "Thank you *so much* for coming!"

Before my head could clear, at least two other board members, as well as the director, expressed similar sentiments. All I could do was shake my head and say a quick word of thanks to an astonishing God who delights in glorifying himself, even through our bungling. He will take even the shakiest faith and use it to bring the light of heaven to the murky shadows of earth.

Grounded for His Glory

Jerry White, popular author and head of the Navigators, delights in the fact that God specializes in using our screwups for His glory. Many years ago White set his heart on becoming an air force pilot. As "a fresh-faced second lieutenant . . . determined to do everything right" on a crucial test in formation flying, everything went wrong:

> As we lifted off the runway, we were caught in the turbulence of the lead jet and thrown into a steep, dangerous bank. We nearly crashed. I was so shaken and tense during the rest of the flight that I flunked the test. Six days later I was out of the program.
>
> "Why?" I cried out to God. Mary, my bride of 18 months, tried to comfort me. We prayed and decided to put our future into God's hands.
>
> To our surprise I was sent to Cape Canaveral, the Air Force Missile Test Center in Florida, as a mission controller in the budding space program, and this changed the entire direction of our lives.

The Whites soon concluded God wanted them to try for a teaching assignment at the U.S. Air Force Academy in Colorado Springs, Colorado, where they could reach cadets for Christ. But several obstacles stood in the way, the major one being Jerry's lack of a master's degree. He applied for admission to the appropriate program, but heard nothing. The couple continued to pray without receiving an answer.

"Then," Jerry writes, "out of the blue, I was asked to speak to a group of generals and colonels." This is what happened next:

> To prepare for the speech, I visited my headquarters in Washington, D.C. There I learned that a sergeant had tossed my school application into a desk drawer. I had not served at Cape Canaveral for the required three years, so I could not attend school. A personnel officer offered to intervene. I declined, saying that as a Christian, I did not want to manipulate

the system, but would leave it in God's hands.

A month later I gave my speech. Afterward a colonel said to me, "Lieutenant, if you ever want to teach at the Air Force Academy, let me know." I was dumbfounded: he was the Academy's director of personnel! Later a colonel told me I was assigned to graduate school, and subsequently I taught at the Academy for six years.[1]

A failed training flight that got him booted from pilot's school became God's chosen means to place Jerry White in the strategic position he now occupies.

How strange is *that?*

The case of the Reluctant Reindeer

Fortunately, it's not only big errors that God reshapes, but little ones as well. Our Lord nurtures an intense interest in the tiniest aspects of our lives — even those non-fatal but terminally embarrassing situations that we stumble into.

Several years ago I served on the volunteer church staff of a youth outreach program. As Christmas approached I was asked to speak at one of our weekly meetings to a couple of hundred high school students, about half of whom had no church connection. I planned to say that Christmas was not about tinsel and elves and Santa and reindeer, but about Jesus Christ. I hoped to make the point in a fun but dramatic way.

While I spoke from the stage to students sitting on the floor below, our sound crew would work from a room near the ceiling on the facing wall. From that spot they could control not only sound, but also spotlights, multimedia productions, and other special effects.

I strung a wire from the sound booth to the stage, and from the wire hung two cardboard reindeer figures, about three feet long apiece. I instructed booth personnel to launch the reindeer toward the stage at a certain point in my talk. As the reindeer glided gracefully over the student's heads, I planned to grab an offstage shotgun (loaded with blanks) and blast the critters from the sky.

Anyway, that was my plan.

At just the right time, the crew launched the reindeer — but the stubborn beasts stalled on the wire, just out of reach of anyone in the booth. Neither jiggling the wire nor shaking it wildly managed to budge my paralyzed reindeer. More vigorous shaking caused the reindeer to lurch ahead, a foot or so at a time. Meanwhile, I had passed the time in my talk where the reindeer were supposed to appear over the heads of the audience. My material was running out!

Just then some students noticed what was happening and started to giggle. I still couldn't grab the gun and fire, however, since these wretched reindeer would fall, unseen, behind the major portion of the crowd. So as I stalled on stage, my reindeer stalled on the wire, and I began to sweat. More and more kids were looking up, pointing, and laughing.

Finally, when I could delay no more, I snatched the gun and shot the reindeer, the crew cut the wire, and my cardboard props fell into the rear of the crowd. It didn't go at all as planned — the graceful reindeer of my imagination had become drunken, cloven-footed clowns.

Just as I reached mid-sentence and panic gripped my throat, a thought occurred. What happened with the reindeer actually fit my talk *better* than what I had planned. I had emphasized that Christmas is about Christ, not reindeer. Our culture has fallen for the Santa stuff because it's slickly packaged, gleaming, and cute. But when you remove the pretty wrapping, you see how deeply stupid it is — not unlike lurching, drunken reindeer. And who could fall in love with such a ridiculous lie, stripped it of its sentimental value?

On the other hand, the real Christmas story stands on its own — smelly stable and all. It doesn't need to be slickly packaged; in fact, it shouldn't be. Cute-ifying it only helps us to miss the point. So that's exactly what I told these suddenly attentive students. I couldn't help but chuckle. What I first feared might collapse into a Yuletide disaster actually made my point better than anything I could have planned.

The God who honors even feeble faith had struck again! And I learned the lesson once more: The Master's unexpected blessings rain out of the sky, even in the form of snockered, *really* red-nosed reindeer!

useful failures

We're all tempted to think that our stumbles, foulups, and blunders automatically disqualify us from having a part in what God wants to do in the hurting world around us. Yes, He may possess limitless power, but how could the Holy One of Israel *stand* us, let alone use us?

When we allow ourselves to descend into such a pit, however, we forget that faith really is stranger than fiction. God delights in taking our silliest, grandest flubs and transforming them by His wisdom and might into trophies of boundless grace.

God isn't looking for perfect people to draft into His army — except for His Son, there aren't any. And He's never depended on the "superstars" to get most of His work done — He knows better than we do that the "giants" walk around on supersized feet of clay. What He's looking for — what He's *always* looking for — are men and women of faith willing to acknowledge their weakness, their sin, their mistakes, and their screwups. With such a rag-tag army, He plans to shake both heaven and earth.

And He might even bring down a few reindeer in the process.

insight from the Bible

It brings us great comfort to think that we serve a God so committed to doling out His love that He enjoys using even our mistakes to advance His kingdom.

But on what ground can we stake such a bold confidence? What biblical evidence can we find to bolster such a hope? Is it really true that, with men and women being what they are — screwups waiting to happen — and God being who He is — the King of the universe who loves to honor even faltering faith — we can expect our Lord to use our mistakes for His glory?

Happily, we don't have to look far to see some potent illustrations of this great truth in the Bible. Let's look at two of the most memorable.

A patriarchal pariah

Consider Abraham. This godly man whom Isaiah calls the friend of God (Isa. 41:8) and whom Paul uses as a preeminent example of faith (see Rom. 4), was no stranger to prat-falls and miscues. And while none of these foulups were good in and of themselves, God used Abraham's very blunders to display His glory to a watching world — and to bless Abraham in spite of himself.

We find the first incident recorded in Genesis 12. Almost immediately after receiving God's promise of blessing, and upon taking his first step of faith by following the Lord's command to leave Ur, Abraham (then Abram) trips on his unbelief in Egypt and falls square on his nose.

Abram knew that his wife, Sarai, turned heads wherever she went. He also knew that the Egyptians recognized a pretty face when they saw one, and that they didn't shrink from slitting the throats of foreign husbands, should the need arise. So Abram asked Sarai to lie for him. "Say you are my sister," he said, "so that I will be treated well for your sake and my life will be spared because of you" (Gen. 12:13).

Sarai did so, and soon Pharaoh himself heard of her beauty. He immediately took her into his own palace. He fell so deeply under her spell that he give Abram "sheep and cattle, male and female donkeys, menservants and maidservants, and camels" (Gen. 12:16).

None of this made the Lord happy. He inflicted serious diseases on Pharaoh and his household — and somehow the king knew why. He summoned Abram and demanded, "What have you done to me? . . . Why didn't you tell me she was your wife? Why did you say, 'She is my sister,' so that I took her to be my wife? Now then, here is your wife. Take her and go!" (Gen. 12:18–19). Pharaoh then "gave orders about Abram to his men, and they sent him on his way, with his wife and everything he had" (Gen. 12:20).

Consider what happened in this sorry incident. Did Abram commit a serious blunder? You bet. Could it have brought disaster? Without question. But God loves being in the business of building our faith. He took Abram's foolish mistake and used it not only to make Abram wealthy, but to reveal to a pagan king the identity of the *real* King.

And here's the really important point to remember: *God continues to work for those who place their faith in Him, even*

when they make the same stupid mistake more than once.
Abraham demonstrates what I mean.

The Abraham of Genesis 20 is no new believer. By then
he is an old man who had walked with God for decades. And
yet, long years after he left Egypt with his tail tucked between
his legs, Abraham moved to a region called Gerar — and immediately retold his lie:

> There Abraham said of his wife Sarah, "She is
> my sister." Then Abimelech king of Gerar sent for
> Sarah and took her. But God came to Abimelech in
> a dream one night and said to him, "You are as good
> as dead because of the woman you have taken; she is
> a married woman" (Gen. 20:2–3).

A terrified Abimelech immediately pleads that he is inno-
cent of wrongdoing, that Abraham had lied to him, and that he
had not touched Sarah. Early the next morning the king summons his advisors, tells them what happened, and soon
everyone's knees are clacking like castanets. Finally Abraham
is subpoenaed to answer the king's accusations:

> "What have you done to us? How have I
> wronged you that you have brought such great guilt
> upon me and my kingdom? You have done things to
> me that should not be done." And Abimelech asked
> Abraham, "What was your reason for doing this?"
> (Gen. 20:9–10).

Abraham responds with the same weak rationale he trot-
ted out in Egypt decades before. Now, don't miss the significance of this: *It's the same stupid blunder he committed many
years earlier.* Except this time, he's known the Lord for years.
He really should know better. Yet instead of what we might
expect — a strong rebuke — this story ends much as did the
lamentable incident by the Nile:

> Then Abimelech brought sheep and cattle and
> male and female slaves and gave them to Abraham,

and he returned Sarah his wife to him. And Abimelech said, "My land is before you; live wherever you like."

To Sarah he said, "I am giving your brother a thousand shekels of silver. This is to cover the offense against you before all who are with you; you are completely vindicated" (Gen. 20:14–16).

Once again Abraham ends up with great riches — and this time, he's even given the right to live wherever he pleases!

It's enough to make you wonder, *Why?* Why does God seem to let Abraham "get away with it" — not once, but twice? My guess is there are at least two reasons.

First, so far as we know, Abraham had no role models for his faith. God broke new ground with this man; Abraham's whole life became a fresh construction site for faith. God used this imperfect instrument to show the world what omnipotence could do with willing dirt (see Ps. 103:14). Yes, Abraham failed, just as we do — we're made of the same stuff he was. But remember that he didn't get away scot-free. Both times God exposed his lie and Abram was dragged, trembling in fear, before an angry king. God used that fear to show Abram that the Lord is the only One who ought to be feared (see Isa. 8:12–14, 51:12–16). And so this "man of faith" finally did learn that trust in God is a much safer and more reliable defense than spineless lies.

Second, consider that the name "Abimelech" is actually a title — something along the lines of "the divine king is my father."[2] God used Abraham's blunder to demonstrate the vast distance between himself and puny man, no matter how lofty the ruler's title. When God told Abimelech, "you are a dead man" (NASB), even the king could not miss the point. God used Abraham's timid faith to sky-write an unmistakable message to the ancient world . . . and to us.

No one should use the ideas in this chapter as an excuse — or worse, as an encouragement — to willfully commit some sin in the mistaken belief that God will use the offense as a launching pad for some strange faith-building exercise. As I write, I can't forget an incident that occurred about eight years ago in my own community.

On a late March morning, an earthquake measuring 5.7 on the Richter scale rocked the Portland, Oregon, area. We had always assumed that earthquakes belonged in California, so the quake came as a bit of a . . . shock. The tremor injured no one and did not cause widespread damage, but it made all of us a little edgy. Suddenly, we were not as earthquake-proof as we thought.

Into this new tectonic awareness stepped John Guntner, a 26-year-old street preacher and computer programmer. Guntner grabbed instant headlines when he prophesied a 10.0 Richter quake would devastate the Portland metropolitan area and much of the Oregon coast. He said the catastrophe would occur on May 3, and that it had been revealed to him by God as he read a passage of Scripture while crossing a local bridge. The judgment, he claimed, came as divine retribution for the unrepentant wickedness of the city.

John's "prophecy" was bad enough, but the pastoral staff of the church he attended copied and sent to more than a thousand area churches a three-page letter Guntner had written warning readers to leave the doomed area. The local media, of course, had a field day. Especially on May 4, when the prophesied quake failed to shake out. Instead, a tribulation of a more familiar nature afflicted Portland: a gentle, soaking rain.

To Guntner's credit, the young man took to the airwaves two days later to discuss his fizzled prediction. He admitted he had been wrong, publicly repented of his recklessness, and asked the people of Portland to forgive him. The Christian talk-show host made it clear that Scripture severely condemned false prophecies and that Guntner had committed an "egregious error," but asked call-in listeners to refrain from casting stones and to welcome Guntner back to the fold.

So far, so good. But an overwhelming number of callers not only excused the would-be prophet's behavior, but approved of it and even *commended* him for it. Sure, the prediction failed, they said — but consider all the evangelism opportunities it created! Look at all the exposure it won for the Lord! Why, the whole city was buzzing; so what if the prediction turned out to be bogus? John Guntner had become a hero!

I couldn't believe my ears. As I listened to caller after caller give rapturous thanks for the incident, I couldn't help but recall the apostle Paul's scorching words in the Book of Romans:

> Someone might argue, "If my falsehood enhances God's truthfulness and so increases his glory, why am I still being condemned as a sinner?" Why not say — as we are being slanderously reported as saying and as some claim that we say — "Let us do evil that good may result"? Their condemnation is deserved (Rom. 3:7–8).

I couldn't help but remember Paul's argument three chapters later, when he indignantly asks, "What shall we say, then? Shall we go on sinning so that grace may increase? By no means! We died to sin; how can we live in it any longer?" (Rom. 6:1–2).

What so many of the callers failed to understand is that God is *not* glorified by willful sin, no matter what "good" might eventually come out of it. This chapter gives no encouragement to:

- abandon one's family
- have an affair (read "commit adultery")
- cheat on one's income tax
- embezzle company funds
- bomb an abortion clinic
- spread malicious gossip
- publicize an imaginary prophecy

. . . or any other conscious, stiff-necked, rebellious, hardhearted, willful sin that might be named.

A first-century foulup

One man does not a pattern make. If Abraham were the only person of faith in Scripture whose bungling got transformed by an Almighty God into an avenue of praise and blessing, this chapter might have been better left unwritten. But the fact is, God seems to specialize in just this kind of strange reversal. Even in the life of someone as highly regarded as the apostle Paul.

All too often we forget Paul's humanity. He messed up, just as we do. While Scripture doesn't highlight for us many of his post-salvation screwups, at least one begs to be noticed.

Shortly after the Jerusalem elders endorsed Paul's preaching of the gospel, the Apostle prepared to set off on another missionary journey. Barnabas, his old friend and mentor, got ready to join him. But sadly, these old friends got into a shouting match which led to a bitter falling out. Here's how Luke tells the sad story:

> Some time later Paul said to Barnabas, "Let us go back and visit the brothers in all the towns where we preached the word of the Lord and see how they are doing." Barnabas wanted to take John, also called Mark, with them, but Paul did not think it wise to take him, because he had deserted them in Pamphylia and had not continued with them in the work. They had such a sharp disagreement that they parted company (Acts 15:36–39).

The root of the conflict is not difficult to identify. Paul — hard-driving, intense, razor-sharp, and mission-driven — lived to bring glory to God by spreading the gospel. Barnabas, on the other hand — easy-going, gentle, highly relational, and people-oriented — loved to bring glory to God by helping others grow toward maturity in Christ.

In other words, you'd want Paul as your professor, but Barnabas as your roommate. They made a great team.

Yet here in Acts 15 we find these two old friends blasting their friendship into smithereens. The Greek word translated "sharp disagreement" is *paroxusmos,* from which we get our word paroxysm, "any sudden, violent outburst, as of action or emotion."[3] In and of itself, this regrettable incident amounted to a setback for the gospel Paul loved and the church Barnabas cherished.

Thank God, however, that faith really is stranger than fiction! For the Lord took this ugly breakup and turned it on its head. As Luke says, "Barnabas took Mark and sailed for Cyprus, but Paul chose Silas and left, commended by the brothers to the grace of the Lord" (Acts 15:39–40).

Prior to this incident, only one dynamic missionary team spread the good news around the Roman world; now a second joined it. Twice as many people would hear the gospel! Eventually the deep wounds slashed open by this ugly disagreement would heal (see 2 Tim. 4:11); but for now God took the very human failings of Paul and Barnabas and used them to glorify himself.

Hope for Today

God loves to take our blunders and use them to glorify himself, to bless His church, and to reach the world. It is precisely this divine tendency that can fill us with hope today. No matter how great our failures of faith, God is greater still!

It's a hard lesson for us to learn, however. Somehow, we often fail to recall God's indignant questions in Isaiah 50:2:

> Was my arm too short to ransom you?
> Do I lack the strength to rescue you?

The answers, of course, are "no" and "no."

It's possible that you may just have blown it big time. You may feel as though your blunder dooms you to a dreary future. But if you are a Christian — if by faith you have entrusted your soul to Christ's tender keeping — it is impossible that any mistake, any blunder, any sin could triumph over His power and love.

Because the truth is, as Isaiah well knew, that God's arms are so long and so bulging with rippling muscle that all the fabric of the universe itself couldn't begin to provide enough material even for a divine warm-up jersey.

Even so, do you worry that one of your mistakes, some of your sins, have put you in God's doghouse? Are you afraid that your awful screwups condemn you to a life on the outskirts of God's love, to a third-rate existence?

If so, put away those fears and douse those worries. Your mistakes can never overshadow the Lord's love and power. If you will just believe and take Him at His word, He will honor your faith — however weak and trembling it might be — and put into motion some strange, new work that will amaze your friends and delight your heart.

According to the Bible, stranger things have happened!

questions for further study

1. Read Psalm 103:1–14.
   A. How is verse 2 a good place to begin thinking about how God uses our mistakes to bring himself glory?
   B. How do verses 10 and 11 give us a strong hope that God will continue to use our errors and even our sins for His glory and our benefit?
   C. How do verses 13 and 14 help us to understand why God loves to use our screwups for His glory? In what ways does this whole passage give us comfort that God isn't done with us yet, even when we've sinned?

2. Read Romans 6:1–14.
   A. What is the basic problem the Apostle addressed in this passage? How does it relate to turning our screwups into divine glory?
   B. Why is it impossible for Paul to believe that anyone would consciously commit sin in order to see God use it for His glory? How does this passage challenge you, personally?
   C. What practical advice does Paul give us in verses 11 through 13? How do you practice this in real life?

3. Read 2 Corinthians 4:17–18.
   A. What view of human nature does Paul reveal in this passage? How does this relate to God using our mistakes for His glory?
   B. Our mistakes and sins can sometimes cause us to lose heart. What advice does Paul give us here for combating those feelings?
   C. What final promise is given to us in verses 16 and 17?
   D. What final advice is given to us in verse 18? How does this entire passage help us to deal with our own humanity?

6

Evil Spelled
Backward Is Live

A friend invited me to his home for a party. The festivities included a videotape of baby boomer memorabilia, including a Roadrunner cartoon. In one brief scene, Wile E. Coyote is set to pull the trigger on a huge catapult loaded with an enormous boulder. He has worked out the rock's trajectory and waits for his nemesis, Roadrunner, to appear. When the bird zooms by, the hapless coyote pulls his rope to fire the catapult . . . but the force of his tug topples the rock directly on his head. He can't win for losing.

I believe God has developed His own form of roadrunner theology. He delights in transforming evil into blockbuster manifestations of His power and wisdom. When evil men and women plot death, our Lord often uses their very evil to bring life.

Faithful believers needn't tremble at the wicked plans of men or devils, for God still rules — and He takes great pleasure in showing the world that faith is stranger than fiction.

Darkness to Light

A few years ago I visited Wheaton, Illinois, to work on a book with the staff of the Chapel of the Air radio ministry. I arrived the day Karen Mains was to record a Christmas message for broadcast on December 25. It gave me chills to hear her tell a remarkable story about how God turns evil inside out in response to the faith of His people.

For many years the city of St. Charles, Illinois, lit up a star of Bethlehem to celebrate the Christmas season. But one day the courts decided the display served to "promote religion" and ordered it discontinued. The town obliged and the night sky went black.

But the following year something strange happened. Two or three large, illuminated stars popped up over businesses and homes where once there had been nothing but air. The next year, several more stars lit up the heavens. Soon hundreds of stars blazed from roofs and windows all over the city, word-lessly proclaiming Jesus' victory of light over darkness and right-eousness over evil.

While in this case I believe the courts mistakenly inter-preted the Constitution, I don't mean to suggest they acted in a consciously evil way. But I *do* mean that they have no jurisdic-tion over the residents of heaven.

Especially the Landlord!

The glowing stars of St. Charles remind me that faith is stranger than fiction, even when evil threatens to blot out the light of heaven. God rules! And no night can grow so dark that a Bethlehem star can't burn a hole clear through it.

One Dictator's Nightmare

Shortly after the fall of the brutal Romanian dictator Nicolae Ceausescu, a good friend of mine traveled through that country with an unusual group of Americans. The little com-pany included nurses, physical therapists, social workers, par-ents of mentally handicapped children, and several severely dis-abled men. The group accompanied the celebrated quadriple-gic author and artist Joni Eareckson Tada.

What made the visit of these Americans so ironic was that for 30 years Ceausescu had told his people, "We have no handi-caps in Romania. Everyone in Romania has whole, healthy bod-ies." Which, being translated, meant that if you had a disability of any sort at all, you were a non-person to be hidden away in an attic or a basement or back room. You were never to appear in public or offend the sensibilities of the "whole-bodied" citizenry enjoying the fruits of Ceausescu's atheistic, worker's paradise.

If you had the misfortune of being *born* with a disability, your prospects were very grim. International relief workers entering the country after the bloody overthrow of the Communist regime were shocked and sickened to find black, unspeakably filthy mediaeval dungeons filled with babies and toddlers judged "imperfect" by the government.

Into this chamber of horrors came a laughing, smiling, singing woman in a power wheelchair, flanked by 40 of the most skilled, loving, caring individuals you could ever hope to load on a single airplane. Once on Romanian soil, the group split up to take their technical skills, boundless compassion, and message of hope in Jesus Christ to the major cities across the country. Slowly at first, almost shyly, and then with a joyous rush, the Romanian people responded to the outreach. Disabled men, women, and children and their families emerged from the attics and basements to attend seminars, church services, and city-wide evangelistic rallies.

My friend will never forget one incident in the northern city of Cluj. Joni's team held an evangelistic rally in one of the city's major indoor sports arenas. Standing-room-only crowds filled the building, while tens of thousands more watched via television. During the traditional greetings, various civic leaders and selected children approached the platform with armloads of flowers for Joni, her husband Ken, and other members of the team. All of this seemed polite and proper and unremarkable . . . until one little boy walked up to the platform all by himself.

Since the little boy lacked arms, he tucked under his chin the single flower he carried for Joni. A hush fell over the audience and — for just a moment — there seemed to be no one else in all the world but one pretty lady in a wheelchair and one small lad who had probably never been seen much in public, let alone on Romanian television.

Joni received the flower, and then smiling through her tears, she turned to the audience. "My little friend and I are going to demonstrate something you may have never seen before. He doesn't have any arms, and my arms are paralyzed. But do you know what? If you have love in your heart, you don't need arms to hug!"

Joni called the boy to her side and — with heads together,

chins over each other's shoulders — demonstrated Romania's first "neck hug." And in that country that had been so cruelly schooled to close its eyes to deformity and close its heart to the humanity of the disabled, two of God's choice children gave a lesson in the triumph of faith.

Ceausescu would not have been pleased. God must have been *very* pleased. "It was," my friend told me, "like a fragile flower poking up through the ashes, for the whole nation to see."

After years of communist evil, the Messiah's gentle, mighty work was beginning to unfold through the "weakest" members of Romanian society.

Later in their Romanian odyssey, Joni and several team members gathered in an ornate conference room in the palatial Hall of Deputies in Bucharest, mere yards away from the upstairs balcony where the dictator used to stand before the masses and praise the virtues of atheistic communism. The Americans met with nine Romanian senators, all of whom soberly asked Joni to pray for them — right then — and for their newly liberated nation. In a strong yet tender voice this severely disabled woman — who just a few months before would have been considered a "non-person" — invoked the blessing of Jesus Christ over the bowed heads of the country's leaders.

How's *that* for turning evil on its head? When God works in response to the faith of His people, you'd better expect some strange things to start happening!

Operation Desert Turnabout

Where faith goes — even in little doses — God is sure to be at work, reversing human evil. Even in places as antagonistic to the gospel as the Middle East.

Saddam Hussein's invasion of Kuwait, for example, actually paved the way for evangelistic success in Iraq. Until then the local Kurdish people remained isolated from the rest of the world, trapped behind formidable barriers — geographic, political, and cultural. Their homeland stretches from eastern Turkey across northern Iraq and into northwestern Iran. The Kurds number about 25 million and had been largely untouched by the gospel.

Until Saddam.

"Before the Gulf War," said one report, "Iraqi Kurdistan had become a slaughterhouse. Saddam's troops waged a vicious genocidal campaign in the restricted area, and the Iraqi dictator instructed his armies to 'leave neither man nor beast alive.' "[1] Somehow, the international community virtually ignored the carnage.

But God didn't.

The U.S. campaign called Operation Desert Storm crippled Saddam's military capabilities and led the following year to the establishment of a security zone in northern Iraq. Following its victory, the American military launched Operation Provide Comfort, one of the largest relief efforts in history.

As food and clothing flooded into the devastated country, concerned Christians built more than four thousand houses for Kurdish war victims. One military insider reported that Christian organizations accounted for more than 90 percent of all relief operations in Iraqi Kurdistan.

And what sort of response did these Christians provoke? "They have been invited to share their faith everywhere," said one source, "and Christian literature is in great demand. One Arabic-speaking evangelist said he recently distributed 172 gospel portions on a street corner in less than 40 minutes, and he added that border agents have asked for their own copies."[2]

Dudley Woodberry of Fuller Seminary's School of World Mission reported that nearly the entire Kurdish town of As-Sulaymaniyah in eastern Iraq began to consider Christianity. He said Kurds there were "rejecting Islam because they don't want a religion capable of producing a tyrant like Saddam Hussein."[3]

Even in Saudi Arabia, the home of Mecca and the heart of the Islamic world, marked changes followed in the wake of the Gulf War. The Bible became more available there than at any time in history — but it took an angry General Norman Schwarzkopf to make it happen. When the U.S. military first asked for Bibles to be allowed into the country to meet the needs of American troops, Saudi officials rejected the request. When Schwarzkopf forcefully objected, Arabic and English-language Bibles began flooding into the country. God's Word arrived on cargo flights where space was available. Perhaps most remarkably, it wasn't unusual to see Third World nationals carrying the distinctive "Desert Storm camouflage" New Testaments on Saudi streets.[4]

Even today, God continues to be at work in the spiritual center of the Muslim world, employing human evil to pave the way for divine blessing. God delights in the faith of His people, and He takes great pleasure in using strange means to show His delight to a watching world.

phosphorous grenades and the gospel

Franklin Graham, head of the Christian relief agency Samaritan's Purse, tells of an unforgettable encounter in Lebanon. Human evil there led directly to the salvation of an entire Lebanese family.

The Hajj clan lived in the village of Aintura, rebuilt after a 1977 shelling. The town sat strategically above a Syrian military encampment. One day the Syrians claimed that a shot from Aintura had been fired at their camp; in response they brutalized the villagers. Soldiers ranged through the town, hurling grenades into shops and houses, incinerating the whole village. When troops found the Hajj family huddled in their kitchen, they tossed a phosphorous grenade into the room and held the door shut to prevent anyone from escaping.

The fire horribly burned all three children, the husband, and the mother, while a grandmother perished in the assault. The mother, Isobelle, was so badly scorched that scar tissue on her arms and hands and chest fused, rendering her arms useless.

And yet — strange as it may seem — God used this evil attack to bring the entire family to faith. The Lord did not prevent evil men from inflicting monstrous pain, but He used even their evil for His own glory. It happened like this.

Just prior to the attack, the family had begun to study the Bible. When the Syrians arrived, the husband, afraid what the newcomers might do, thought it wisest to discontinue their reading. His decision saddened Isobelle, since she was beginning to understand and believe in Christ, but she complied. After the attack, the family not only accepted the depravity of man as taught in the Scriptures, but also laid hold of the hope of the gospel. All placed their faith in Christ.

Still, there was the tragedy of Isobelle's useless arms. What could be done? Graham eventually persuaded one of the top plastic surgeons in the country to take up Isobelle's case. Over the course of a full year, the surgeon restored mobility to her arms. An overjoyed Isobelle wrote a letter to Graham:

> I took this pen with a trembling hand, not trembling from fear — but from joy and happiness, which is the first letter since my operation, which by the mercy of the Lord and your kindness has helped to restore. . . . Truly I had to suffer a lot during this year, but deep inside me I have had joy and comfort. And when I was alone, I always used to repeat in my heart why God has permitted this to happen. It was the door for our salvation and eternal life.[5]

Can anyone honestly claim that faith is *not* stranger than fiction?

Like and Trust Aren't the Same

Let's admit it, nobody likes to suffer. Whether or not we're privileged to see God respond to our faith in wonderfully strange ways, suffering *hurts*. It isn't on anyone's top ten list of things to do. We don't like it when evil men and women cause us pain — and God doesn't ask us to like it.

What He *does* ask us to do is to trust Him. Because faith is stranger than fiction, God wants us to focus on His power, not our troubles; on His love, not our pain. Without denying either our troubles or our pain, God asks us to look to Him for help and deliverance.

In other words, stop looking at the clouds and begin watching for the sun. In faith, expect that somehow God will reverse the *evil* and turn it into a beautiful new way for you to *live*.

Insight from the Bible

No doubt all of us enjoy stories about criminals whose evil acts bite them in the leg. I know that I chuckled when I read about Edilber Guimaraes, a 19-year-old Brazilian arrested for attempted theft in a glue factory. It seems that when the young man stopped to sniff some of the glue he was trying to steal, he tipped over two large cans of adhesive. When police arrived at the factory, they found the immobilized Guimaraes stuck fast to the floor.[6]

Such a scene unavoidably reminds me of Psalm 73:18–20:

> Surely you place them [the wicked] on slippery ground; you cast them down to ruin. How suddenly are they destroyed, completely swept away by terrors! As a dream when one awakes, so when you arise, O LORD, you will despise them as fantasies.

Don't consider this mere Jewish rhetoric; the words remain as true today as when they were penned thousands of years ago. The evil plans of the wicked can still blow away in an instant. And sometimes, God honors the faith of His children by transforming evil conspiracies into highways of blessing for the feet of the oppressed.

what's Deeper than a well?

I'm pretty sure I understand what Isaiah meant in the passage I just quoted, but not all Scripture seems so immediately clear. Consider a little verse in the Book of Hebrews, for example. It always struck me a little odd that the writer of Hebrews 11 chose to honor the Old Testament patriarch Joseph with the following words:

> By faith Joseph, when his end was near, spoke about the exodus of the Israelites from Egypt and gave instructions about his bones (Heb. 11:22).

About his *bones*? I mean, *who cares*? Had I been assigned to edit his manuscript, I probably would have written a memo to the following effect:

Dear contributor:
  Hi! I just wanted to take this opportunity to

thank you for all the hard work you've put in on your part of the Bible project. The whole thing is shaping up nicely, and I think your contribution is one of its highlights. Congratulations!

I love the way you set the tone for the book. Your majestic portrait of the Son takes away my breath, and the way you compare and contrast the new covenant with the old looks excellent. Great job!

I've already written to you about some problems that I think readers might have with chapters 6 and 10. It'd be no good to make people scratch their heads and wonder just exactly what you mean! But I'm sure you'll take care of all of that. Thanks for your prompt attention to the matter.

I do have one more teensy suggestion to make. The manuscript looks great overall, but . . . what were you thinking in 11:22? The life of Joseph takes up almost a full 30 percent of the Book of Genesis — 14 out of 50 chapters — and you highlight his *funeral arrangements*? I'd really like you to rethink this. Genesis describes many powerful incidents in Joseph's life that would better illustrate his deep faith. Why'd you pick bones, anyway? Look, if the deadline is too stressful for you, we could move it back a few weeks. I'd rather do that and have a bestseller on our hands than push to meet the schedule and wind up with . . . well, bones.

Do you see what I mean? I'm anxious to speak with you about this. Call me when you get the chance.

Meanwhile, thanks for a *super* effort. With a little more work, this manuscript could really go places!

> Sincerely in Him,
> Stephanos

It's a good thing I wasn't in the publishing business two thousand years ago. The way it stands, Hebrews 11:22 demonstrates an ingenious aspect of Scripture. The Bible seems to leave some things deliberately unclear for the simple reason that God wants us to sweat a little before we come up with "the answer." This technique separates the men from the boys, the genuinely interested from the merely curious. Jesus did it all the time with His parables. Those who really want to know what God means in a perplexing text will dig until they hit pay dirt; those who think of the Bible as a religious Trivial Pursuit game will pass and move on to more "exciting" categories.

I now think the Bible mentions Joseph's burial details as a shorthand way of calling to mind the patriarch's sterling character, as well as his amazing prophetic career. God doesn't hand out prophecies of the central event of the Old Testament — the exodus — to just anybody. This reference in Hebrews reminds us just what an immense figure Joseph was, and that he remained faithful to God until his dying day.

Had the writer of Hebrews chosen to dwell on a more extended incident from Joseph's life, however, he may well have decided to highlight a text from Genesis 50. A verse in that chapter has often comforted God's people during times of human brutality. But before I quote it, perhaps I should briefly rehearse where Joseph had been before the Holy Spirit prompted him to utter those soothing words.

Joseph was his father's pet. Jacob never even tried to hide his favoritism from his other sons; in fact, he flaunted it by lavishing on Joseph special gifts and treatment. No wonder Joseph's brothers hated him and decided to make him disappear!

One day they saw Joseph approaching and a hateful plan began to take shape in their minds. They attacked him, stripped him, and threw him down a well, then debated his fate. Trapped in this deep, dark hole, Joseph had to wonder how much further his fortunes could sink. *Not much deeper,* he may have thought.

Wrong.

His brothers sold him as a slave to a group of roving merchants, and for the next several years, whenever things began to look up for Joseph, his world came crashing down. He lurched from a position of favor to a jail cell, from a chance at freedom to continued imprisonment. God seemed to be nowhere. . . .

Until it was God's time.

In a swift turn of events utterly characteristic of the way

God often operates in response to the faith of His loved ones, Joseph rose to become the second most powerful man in Egypt. Eventually the brothers who betrayed him landed in his hands. He could do to them what he willed. Kill them? Torture them? Enslave them? Let them go free? The terrified brothers sweat bullets. Who wouldn't? But Joseph spoke to them kindly:

> You intended to harm me, but God intended it
> for good to accomplish what is now being done, the
> saving of many lives (Gen. 50:20).

Above all, Joseph wanted to please his heavenly Master. He knew that God ruled, not the evil choices of wicked men. And Joseph also knew God loved to show His power by using the worst men could do to bring about great good.

God overruled the whole mess. He took undeniably evil acts and turned them inside out to His everlasting glory . . . but He also allowed one of His choice servants to remain in the dark (figuratively and literally) for a very long time.

God often seems to work in ways very like this. In fact, He might be at work in your life right now in just this fashion. You could be locked in some prison this moment — whether of walls and bars or of emotional chains, it makes little difference — and are wondering why God doesn't seem interested in rescuing you. You might even be wondering, *Can God do it? Is He able to rescue me from my enemy's hands?*

Joseph's story teaches us that God still sits on the throne of the universe. He doesn't find it hard at all to reverse human evil. It doesn't challenge Him in the least. We should never imagine that He strains to figure out how to use the actions of wicked people to further His holy purposes. One of my favorite authors, John Piper, puts it like this:

> People lift their hand to rebel against the Most
> High only to find that their rebellion is unwitting ser-
> vice in the wonderful designs of God. Even sin can-
> not frustrate the purposes of the Almighty.

Similarly, when we come to the end of the New Testament and to the end of history in the Revelation of John, we find God in complete control of all the evil kings who wage war. In Revelation 17, John speaks of a harlot sitting on a beast with ten horns.

The harlot is Rome, drunk with the blood of the saints; the beast is the antichrist and the ten horns are ten kings "who give over their power and authority to the beast . . . [and] make war on the Lamb."

But are these evil kings outside God's control? Are they frustrating God's designs? Far from it. They are unwittingly doing his bidding. "For God has put it in their hearts to carry out his purpose by being of one mind and giving their royal power to the beast, until the words of God shall be fulfilled" (Rev. 17:17). No one on earth can escape the sovereign control of God: "The king's heart is a stream of water in the hand of the Lord; he turns it wherever he will" (Prov. 21:1;RSV; compare Ezra 6:22).[7]

At the beginning of his trials, Joseph probably wondered if he could descend any deeper than the well into which his brothers dumped him. Then he found out the answer — yes, it could get deeper. Much deeper. First there was slavery. Then exile into Egypt. Then false accusations. Then prison for at least two years. When Joseph finally reached the bottom of the pit, to his amazement he discovered something deeper still. Curiously, however, he had to look up to see it.

They say that at the bottom of a very deep well, you can see stars. If that's true, then Joseph saw myriad galaxies all blazing with unquenchable light. Perhaps that's what helped him keep going in those long years when everything he did seemed to turn out wrong. Deep in the pit he looked up, saw God's stars, and knew that the same limitless power that placed those stars in the heavens could also lift him to high places. The deepest thing of all in Joseph's life was the wisdom and love of God.

The same is true for you. Faith is stranger than fiction — even when you come face to face with the evil deeds of wicked men and women. God loves to honor your faith by taking human evil and turning it inside out for His glory and our blessing.

But remember, He does it most often in strange, unexpected ways! I agree wholeheartedly with the poem my sister Barb wrote several years ago:

> I went to the door for Routine
> And found Unexpected there.
> It loomed tall and large, and mean,
> And filled me with terrible care.
>
> It entered and carried me with it
> To all imagined places of woe.
> 'Til my Lord said, "Wait just a minute —
> You're not alone, I've told you so!
>
> "Wherever it takes you, I'm with you.
> I'll walk with you, right by your side.
> Whatever you have to go through,
> With you I will always abide."
>
> He traveled with me through the valley,
> And was there when I came back once more.
> He sent others to help my soul rally,
> Encouraging my spirit to soar.
>
> Routine is always the known way;
> We like to take that route alone.
> Give thanks for the Unexpected pathway —
> The detour leads right to the Throne.
> — BJL

Questions for further study

1. Read Psalm 73.
   A. How is the Psalmist's reaction to human evil in verses 2, 3, 13, and 14 often like our own? Why do we react this way (verses 4–12)?
   B. What is the danger of focusing too long on the thoughts mentioned in verses 13 and 14 (verse 15)?
   C. How did the Psalmist get his thinking straightened out (verses 16–17)? How did this cause a change in his thinking? Can it do the same for us? Explain.

    D. What realization finally hit the Psalmist (verses 18–20)?

    E. In what way did the Psalmist change his outlook (verses 21–28)? How do his words reflect a belief that faith is stranger than fiction?

2. Read Genesis 50:19–20.

    A. What does this passage teach about how God loves to "reverse" human evil in response to the faith of His people?

    B. Why is it significant that these words were spoken by Joseph, with his particular personal history?

3. Read 2 Kings 19:14–37.

    A. Describe the situation outlined in this passage. Who is involved? What is the danger? Why is God's "strange" help so required here? Describe how God responded to the faith of His people.

    B. How does God react to the haughty words of the evil king? How does His reaction never change to such a display of pride?

    C. Verse 34 gives the bedrock reason why God loves to "reverse" human evil in response to the faith of His people. What is it?

7

Righteous Reversals

Just when you think you have this business of faith-is-stranger-than-fiction figured out, our amazing God does something else that completely blows your circuits. Just when you think you can guess how God will act in a certain situation, POOF! He honors your faith in a totally unexpected way.

Naturally, these "righteous reversals" usually take us by surprise. And they don't always come with a "happily-ever-after" ending.

Even This Qualifies

One Sunday at church I attended a "parent dedication" service. Six couples brought their children forward so that we might pray for the strength, stamina, and wisdom each couple would need to rear their children. The event proceeded as most do, with some laughter and some tears, some nervousness and some profound insights. But the usual routine came to an abrupt end when the last of the couples presented their daughter.

Their one-year-old child, they explained, was born deaf and partially blind. With just half a brain, neurologists said she couldn't develop mentally past two months of age. She was fed through a tube, since she never learned to swallow. The couple had an older son (healthy) and was expecting another baby in a few months (we prayed for healthy). They weren't sure how far they ought to go medically to keep their daughter alive.

After the mother fully explained their heartbreak, the

father spoke. "I have the same kind of deformity my daughter has," he said, "except mine is in my heart. Sin has affected her physically — my problem is spiritual."

Then he stopped to collect himself and describe the work of a faith-honoring God. No, the Lord didn't miraculously heal his daughter on the platform and, no, his whole extended family, neighborhood, city, county, and state didn't come to faith because of the heartbreak.

"But one good thing has come out of all this," he said while we all wiped away hot tears. "My wife and I have grown much closer together. I've grown a lot closer to God and have learned to depend upon Him completely."

Then this courageous couple turned around and joined the other parents behind the pulpit, waiting for the church to pray for them. Believe me, we prayed! And I know to whom we prayed.

Not to the God of our fantasy. Not to the God of never-never land. But to the God who honors our faith by turning even the most heart-wrenching tragedies into bits of divine glory.

And as I sat moist-eyed in the pew, I thought, *even this qualifies.*

A Ray of sunshine

I'm glad that not all righteous reversals spark bittersweet emotions. Many taste just plain sweet.

Ray Holder is the father of one of my good friends, as well as a hospital chaplain. Someone in Ray's position sees more heartache, ecstasy, sorrow, and exhilaration in one year than most of us witness in a lifetime. Hospital chaplains ride a constant roller coaster of emotions, from stratospheric highs to mine-shaft lows. But they're also privileged to witness many glorious righteous reversals.

One Monday morning a patient on the fifth floor asked Ray to stop by. Only a few minutes into the visit, the patient blurted out, "How can I be a real Christian, Chaplain?" The question both surprised and delighted Ray, and the chaplain led the man to a saving relationship with Christ. The patient then explained he had been praying all night for himself and the man in the next room, who he said "was in very bad shape."

"As I left that room," Ray recalls, "one of our Christian nurses rejoiced with me over our friend's salvation and said, 'I want you to see two others.' One of them was the man in the next room, suffering from emphysema; he was listed in serious condition. This ex-logger swore every other word, even when unconscious. His Christian nephew was there. We talked. I then spoke with the ex-logger and he seemed to understand. I briefly explained God's plan of salvation and prayed as he listened. When I asked him if he was trusting the Lord as his Savior, he said, 'No — go on.' I said I'd keep praying for him, talked briefly with his nephew, and left the room as he fell back into cursing again."

Ray immediately found the nurse and described his encounter to her. She said she knew the man and would talk to him. As the nurse spoke clearly, lovingly, and tenderly to the dying logger, Ray visited an elderly woman unsure of her eternal destiny. While Ray went to work in one room and the nurse in the other, God labored in both rooms simultaneously, using even illness for His glory.

"Both of these individuals prayed that morning to confess their sin to God and to place their faith in Jesus Christ as their very own personal Savior and Lord!" Ray said. "The elderly woman read a prayer in a little booklet that I had given her and signed her name and date, then wrote underneath her signature, 'I love you, Lord!' The ex-logger died later that evening. The next week his wife also became a believer in Christ as her neighbors — a retired pastor and his wife — lovingly cared for her and helped her in her grief. There were tears of joy on the fifth floor that day and in heaven, rejoicing over the salvation of these precious and special individuals."

Of course, righteous reversals aren't reserved for salvation experiences alone; God may also use them in the lives of His beloved children.

One dear Christian lady approached Ray about her own illness: "Chaplain, I've been a Christian for many years. God has been so good to me in so many ways. I'm thankful — but it seems like I've been sick for over 40 years! My body is all out of balance now and they just can't seem to tell what is causing all these problems. I'm so discouraged — I just don't know what to do!"

Ray prayed with the woman before leaving her room, but it wasn't until the drive home later that evening that Paul's words about a "thorn" in his flesh came to mind. When he got home, Ray looked up those famous verses in 2 Corinthians 12:7–10. He also saw that week's issue of *Moody Monthly* lying on his kitchen table. The following paragraph by Joni Eareckson Tada caught his attention:

> People with disabilities are God's best visual aids to demonstrate who He really is. His power shows up best in weakness. And who, by the world's standards, is weaker than the mentally or physically disabled? As the world watches, these people persevere. They live, love, trust, and obey him. Eventually, the world is forced to say, "How great their God must be to inspire this kind of loyalty."

Later that evening Ray called his sick friend and told her what he had learned. The next day her attitude seemed much improved, and when she was discharged from the hospital, she repeatedly thanked the chaplain for calling her that night.

Now, I know this kind of righteous reversal isn't likely to make the evening news or even Sunday's sermon — but it's a reversal nevertheless, bringing glory to God and hope to His downcast people. Who else but God could bring spiritual life out of death and spiritual health out of disease?

smiles All Around

Some time ago I read about a righteous reversal that just made me smile. The article described the Metawwa, an 8,000-member religious police force in Saudi Arabia that claims to answer to Allah alone. This group decided it was time to clamp down hard on Christian activity and scheduled a secret meeting in Riyadh on how to identify and disrupt Christian activities in the country, how to stake out and report on Christian gatherings, and how to collect rewards.

But the Metawwa made a crucial mistake: It forgot that faith is stranger than fiction.

It invited to the meeting a Sudanese man whom the

Metawwa assumed was a Muslim. Not so. The man was a dedicated Christian whom God immediately enlisted in the F.B.I. (the Father's Bureau of Infiltration). So, "as a consequence of this divinely arranged infiltration, Christian fellowships in recent months have been able to take protective countermeasures."[1]

In other words, a clandestine meeting designed to cause trouble for Christians instead turned into a vehicle for their protection. Why? Because God loves to honor the faith of his people — and He also delights in surprises.

Welcome once more to the topsy-turvy world of righteous reversals!

winning at spiritual warfare

What the devil intends for ill, God uses for good. This became clear once again at a seminar of the Institute in Basic Life Principles, held in Seattle. Five thousand attendees gawked as a young man ran up on stage and attempted to disrupt the meeting. "What followed," said an IBLP newsletter, "demonstrated the mighty power of God." It also illustrated His fondness for righteous reversals.

Leaders immediately ushered the young man backstage and entered into a 20-minute battle of spiritual warfare. At the end of that time, the man broke free from strongholds of bitterness and immorality. When this young man and his father were asked to give the audience a testimony of praise to God, they said yes.

Leaders immediately paused the meeting and, to the delight and amazement of the crowd, this father and son walked out onto the stage where just moments before the evil one had tried to wreck the seminar. Except this time the happy pair told how God had freed the young man from the bondage of Satan.[2]

That's what happens when God, always eager to reward the faith of His people, brings about a righteous reversal. Our Lord froze the evil in its tracks and reversed it, to the glory of His matchless name.

from seattle to vietnam

All over the world and in the lives of countless of His precious children, God demonstrates His desire to honor and increase our faith by reversing Satan's evil schemes before they can take root.

A story from Vietnam illustrates God's fondness for righteous reversals. Communist leaders had learned that Christianity was exploding in an area where an evangelist had been preaching. Party officials became so alarmed they dispatched several "teachers" to conduct a six-hour "re-education campaign" in the village. Here's what happened next:

> At the end of the session, one of the officials strode to the blackboard and scribbled two headings: "Against Christ" and "For Christ." He then asked the villagers to write their names in the appropriate column. The people sat motionless as they pondered how to respond.
>
> Finally, an elderly woman who had previously served as a Marxist spokesperson in the village addressed the group. "For the past 20 years I have followed Marxism," she said. "I have followed the party line and served as your leader. But a few months ago, I came to realize that Jesus Christ offers a better way." She then signed her name as one who was "For Christ." As the chagrined cadres watched, the entire village took her cue and followed suit.[3]

How can you read such an account and not break into a smile? God took a potential disaster and, in response to the faith of a new believer, transformed it into an overpowering witness for the truth of the gospel. And so He placed at center stage a faithful woman who formerly led the opposition!

But it gets even better. If you're not smiling now, I think the corners of your mouth will rise in a few moments. This is how the report concludes:

> A denominational field representative familiar with this account reports that government officials are baffled by the move of God in the area. He relates that an . . . article translated from a Vietnamese newspaper concluded: "We don't know what is hap-

pening, but it is something called the 'Good News' religion."

Good news? You bet! Good news that Jesus Christ took on human flesh, died for our sins, and rose from the dead, never to die again. Good news that we can enter into His life through faith in His name. Good news that He still sits at the helm of the universe, continually searching for those who will cast their futures in His hands. And yes, good news that sometimes His actions baffle human understanding. And that includes Christians.

We, too, can be mystified by what God does. But we should never be *completely* surprised. For although His methods often change, His character never does. And that's why, this side of heaven, we can live in the confidence that faith will always be stranger than fiction.

present-Day Reversals

Righteous reversals aren't possible until the sky grows inky black. God allows wickedness to smack its lips over a dish of roasted saints just before the Heavenly Health Department moves in, closes down the violator, and sets out a banquet table for the faithful.

Because God is an expert at righteous reversals, He knows just when they're needed and so brings them out of His store-house at precisely the right time.

It may be that you need such a reversal right now. The darkness is closing in and you lack any power to dispel the gloom. My friend, while I can't guarantee that God will perform a righteous reversal on your behalf, I do know that He will act in exactly the right way at precisely the best hour. He doesn't leave your life to chance; He'll never leave you dangling in the wind. God wants you to trust that He *will* deliver you.

But He also wants you to remember that the *how* of His deliverance and His timing can never be clearly predicted!

So do me this favor, would you? Should the Lord stretch out His mighty hand and turn upside down some evil scheme that threatens your world — should He prove to you again that faith is stranger than fiction — then take a few moments alone to praise the Lord of glory. And then open your mouth in public adoration, so others may stand amazed at the God who honors simple faith in such strange but beautiful ways.

Insight from the Bible

Perhaps the clearest biblical example of a righteous reversal is the remarkable account found in the Book of Esther. For in this incident, instead of using the evil for His glory, God reversed it altogether. Satan never put a glove on God's people; in effect, Lucifer bloodied his lip with a clear shot to his own jaw.

But it didn't start out that way.

From Head Advisor to Dead Downsizer

The events described in Esther took place following Israel's 70 years of captivity in Babylon. Although some Jews returned to their homeland after Cyrus conquered Babylon in 539 B.C., many remained scattered throughout the vast Persian empire. Among those Jews was Esther, the beautiful young cousin of Mordecai. Esther grew up as an orphan, and Mordecai reared her as his own. The story pulsates with irony and overflows with illustrations of God's providence; only a thorough reading of the book does it justice. But allow me to briefly recap the highlights.

Esther's stunning good looks inevitably attracted the attention of the royal palace, and when she won a nationwide beauty contest, she became queen. At almost the same time, Mordecai overheard a plot to assassinate the king. He reported it to Esther, who informed Xerxes. Scribes faithfully recorded Mordecai's allegiance in the official palace archives.

Some time later Haman, who enjoyed "a seat of honor higher than that of all the other nobles" (Esther 3:1), grew furious with Mordecai for a perceived snub. Immediately he began to plot vengeance:

> When Haman saw that Mordecai would not
> kneel down or pay him honor, he was enraged. Yet

having learned who Mordecai's people were, he scorned the idea of killing only Mordecai. Instead Haman looked for a way to destroy all Mordecai's people, the Jews, throughout the whole kingdom of Xerxes (Esther 3:5–6).

Soon Haman convinced the king that it would be in his best interest to eradicate the Jews. Dispatches flew to all corners of the kingdom "with the order to destroy, kill, and annihilate all Jews — young and old, women and little children — on a single day, the thirteenth day of the twelfth month, the month of Adar, and to plunder their goods" (Esther 3:13).

When Mordecai heard the news, he tore his clothes, donned sackcloth and ashes, and wailed bitterly. Esther, who had not received word of the king's edict, became alarmed when she learned of her uncle's behavior. After receiving a full report, she and her uncle came up with a plan of action based on a piece of vital information unknown to Haman: Esther, too, was a Jew.

Part of the plan called for Esther to invite both Xerxes and Haman to a series of lavish banquets. The king loved this royal treatment and promised Esther he would grant her fondest wish; but Esther kept her request to herself until just the right moment. The invitation also thrilled Haman so much that he boasted to his friends:

> "I'm the only person Queen Esther invited to accompany the king to the banquet she gave. And she has invited me along with the king tomorrow. But all this gives me no satisfaction as long as I see that Jew Mordecai sitting at the king's gate."
>
> His wife Zeresh and all his friends said to him, "Have a gallows built, seventy-five feet high, and ask the king in the morning to have Mordecai hanged on it. Then go with the king to the dinner and be happy." This suggestion delighted Haman, and he had the gallows built (Esther 5:12–14).

That night the king could not sleep. He ordered that the record of his administration be read to him, and soon he heard again of Mordecai's part in exposing the assassination plot. It displeased Xerxes to learn that nothing had been done to honor the man who had saved his life. Just then Haman entered the outer court of the palace, intending to ask that Mordecai be hanged. The king invited Haman into the throne room and wondered aloud what ought to be done for someone the king wanted to highly honor. Haman assumed he must be the one to be rewarded, and so answered:

> For the man the king delights to honor, have them bring a royal robe the king has worn and a horse the king has ridden, one with a royal crest placed on its head. Then let the robe and horse be entrusted to one of the king's most noble princes. Let them robe the man the king delights to honor, and lead him on the horse through the city streets, proclaiming before him, "This is what is done for the man the king delights to honor!" (Esther 6:7–9).

The king thought the idea splendid and ordered Haman to carry out his plan immediately — in honor of Mordecai the Jew.

A humiliated Haman did as he was told, then rushed home and spilled the awful news to his wife and friends. They all saw the handwriting on the wall: "Since Mordecai, before whom your downfall has started, is of Jewish origin, you cannot stand against him — you will surely come to ruin!" (Esther 6:13).

And so Round One came to an end in this Old Testament righteous reversal. Round Two — a decisive one — would begin immediately.

No sooner had Haman poured out his grief than he had to run off to Esther's banquet. King Xerxes again pled to know what his beloved queen might request of him. This time, she answered:

> If I have found favor with you, O king, and if it pleases your majesty, grant me my life — this is my petition. And spare my people — this is my request. For I and my people have been sold for destruction

and slaughter and annihilation. If we had merely been sold as male and female slaves, I would have kept quiet, because no such distress would justify disturbing the king (Esther 7:3–4).

The king exploded in anger and demanded to know who would dare to threaten his lovely queen. "The adversary and enemy is this vile Haman," Esther replied (Esther 7:6).

Xerxes arose in a rage and stalked off to his garden. Haman felt the hangman's noose tightening around his neck and stayed behind to beg Esther for his life. Just as he threw himself on her royal couch, Xerxes returned. "Will he even molest the queen while she is with me in the house?" he stormed. The final words of chapter seven mark the official end of Round Two:

> As soon as the word left the king's mouth, they covered Haman's face. Then Harbona, one of the eunuchs attending the king, said, "A gallows seventy-five feet high stands by Haman's house. He had it made for Mordecai, who spoke up to help the king."
>
> The king said, "Hang him on it!" So they hanged Haman on the gallows he had prepared for Mordecai. Then the king's fury subsided (Esther 7:8–10).

Only one problem remained. The king's edict to destroy the Jews could not be rescinded, since "no document written in the king's name and sealed with his ring can be revoked" (Esther 8:8). But another decree could be issued, one giving the Jews the right to defend themselves. That order was given and suddenly a new day had dawned:

> For the Jews it was a time of happiness and joy, gladness and honor. In every province and in every city, wherever the edict of the king went, there was joy and gladness among the Jews, with feasting and celebrating. And many people of other nationalities became Jews because fear of the Jews had seized them (Esther 8:16–17).

Time to check your scorecards, boxing fans. Round Three is over, the knockout punch has been delivered. And a classic righteous reversal is in the books. The *New Bible Commentary* sums it up as well as anyone:

> In an unforseeable way, circumstances so fell out that Haman became the victim of his own plot, the Jews were delivered, their enemies were liquidated, and a Jew [Mordecai] was appointed to the position of greatest influence next to the king. This miraculous reversal of affairs was celebrated throughout the Persian Empire, and is still celebrated annually by Jews in every part of the world at the festival known as Purim.[4]

Because faith is stranger than fiction, it deserves to be heartily celebrated. Long live Purim!

Reverses with a Twist

As we've noted, not all righteous reversals boast a "happily ever after" ending. And yet they still deserve mention in the "Truth is stranger than fiction" Hall of Fame.

Consider for a moment how God sometimes deals with the illnesses and other physical woes that beset His children. They come at us from nowhere, cause us great pain, and sometimes prompt us to doubt God's love.

Now, I am deeply grateful that God still heals and that He continues to miraculously cure "incurable" diseases. But He doesn't always do so and — surprising as it may seem — we ought to be grateful that He doesn't. I'm sure the people of Galatia would agree.

The power-packed Book of Galatians heads up a train of Pauline letters hitched to the apostle's "major" epistles of Romans and First and Second Corinthians. Sometimes it's called "little Romans" because it explores the theme of justification by faith, not by works. Except for a mysterious disease, however, we likely never would have enjoyed its liberating wisdom. That might sound strange, but Paul himself explains what I mean:

As you know, it was because of an illness that I first preached the gospel to you. Even though my illness was a trial to you, you did not treat me with contempt or scorn. Instead, you welcomed me as if I were an angel of God, as if I were Christ Jesus himself (Gal. 4:13–14).

The logic seems inescapable to me: without the illness, Paul would not have preached to the Galatians; had Paul not preached to the Galatians, they would not have come under his care; had they not come under his care, he would not have written them a letter; and had he not written them a letter, we could not read Galatians today.

It doesn't matter what kind of illness Paul suffered. The point is that God used a repulsive physical condition — a "trial" to the Galatians that might well have produced "contempt" or "scorn" — and used it to bring the gospel to those who hadn't heard it (and a portion of Scripture to the church which needs it).

Faith is stranger than fiction — and God can use tools as microscopic as viruses and bacteria in shaping us for glory.

Thorns and Roses

Franklin L. Stanton held definite ideas about roses and thorns, and his opinion probably represents the majority:

> This world that we're a-livin in
> is mighty hard to beat;
> You git a thorn with every rose,
> But *ain't* the roses *sweet!*"[5]

Most of us consider the bloom delightful and the thorn unfortunate. I do! But in the topsy-turvy world of righteous reversals, the thorn sometimes *is* the bloom. That's what Paul discovered through another divinely ordained personal trial.

The Corinthians presented real problems for the Apostle. Of all the churches Paul planted, this one gave him the most trouble. That's why we have two letters to the Corinthians in our New Testament; the first book didn't come close to straightening out the mess, and in the second Paul warns the church that he's on his way to take care of matters personally.

This church apparently refused to take Paul seriously. Many in the congregation simply dismissed the Apostle's authority. So beginning with chapter 10 of 2 Corinthians, Paul begins to build the case for his apostleship. For two full chapters he details his divine commission, his ceaseless labors, his deep concern for the church, and his battle scars. By the time he reaches chapter 12, he's describing a heavenly vision he received. He does all of this to defend his authority as a minister of the gospel. But a shift of tone occurs in verse 7:

> To keep me from becoming conceited because of these surpassingly great revelations, there was given me a thorn in my flesh, a messenger of Satan, to torment me. Three times I pleaded with the Lord to take it away from me. But he said to me, "My grace is sufficient for you, for my power is made perfect in weakness" (2 Cor. 12:7-9).

God refused Paul's request for deliverance, not because of a deficiency in the Apostle's faith, but because the Lord intended to use the malady (whatever it was) for His own glory. The gospel would be better served *with* the thorn than *without* it.

I think it's unfortunate that we don't generally celebrate the rest of Paul's comments as his phrase about God's power being made perfect in weakness. Paul himself emphasized the very thing we overlook:

> Therefore I will boast all the more gladly about my weaknesses, so that Christ's power may rest on me. That is why, for Christ's sake, I delight in weaknesses, in insults, in hardships, in persecutions, in difficulties. For when I am weak, then I am strong (2 Cor. 12:9–10).

Don't skip too fast to the "when I am weak, then I am strong" part. Linger over the preceding sentences. Paul claims that the *only* reason Christ's power rested on him was because of his weakness. In that case, it makes perfect sense for him to "delight in weaknesses, in insults, in hardships, in persecutions, in difficulties," because those are the very things that qualify him to become a conduit of divine energy. Insult Paul? Fine! He gets power. Persecute him? Great! He gets power.

Paul didn't like thorns any more than we do, but he finally came to see that sometimes thorns bless us more than blossoms. The Apostle intended to pop Satan's balloon, and he knew a thorn would do the trick a lot quicker than a petal.

Is That a Thorn in Your Foot?

Some righteous reversals seem easier to take than others, don't they? If someone were to walk up to me and ask, "Steve, do you delight in weaknesses, in insults, in hardships, in persecutions, in difficulties? Because, you know, only when you're weak will you be strong," I might very well respond with a kick to the kneecap and a "Well, brother, as you can see, I am better at giving them than taking them. By the way, do *you* feel stronger now?"

None of us likes to think about the thorns that may invade our lives. And I believe this aversion is normal and even healthy. I have yet to find a single biblical text that tells me to pray for thorns.

Thorns come into our lives unbidden, however. We don't have to ask for them! And when we request that they be taken away, the answer is sometimes no.

It's exactly at that point that the Apostle's teaching is meant for us. Learn it now; apply it then. But don't buzz around foisting your biblical expertise on everyone in sight. Few things feel as obnoxious as someone with steel-toed boots lecturing a barefooted thorn-bearer that he really ought to thank God for his blood soaking the ground.

Even so, *all* righteous reversals illustrate that faith is stranger than fiction. And that remains true, even when tragedy strikes. It is this conviction that can sustain you when you find yourself in the middle of a terrible trial. God has not lost control! He does not despise your faith, however feeble and wavering it might be. It may be that He plans to use Satan's worst afflictions to honor your trust and bring himself glory.

And remember: Most of the time, He gets that glory through you.

Questions for further study

1. Read Daniel 6.
    A. Describe the trap Daniel's enemies set for him. How did this prepare the way for what God was about to do?
    B. On what does the king focus in his question of verse 20? How is this question often a focus for divine activity?
    C. How does this righteous reversal conclude? How does it compare to Esther's experience?
    D. What does the king's decree, recorded in verses 26 and 27, teach us about how God responds to genuine faith? How does verse 26 illustrate the foundation for all of God's work on our behalf?

2. Read Acts 18:9–17.
    A. What was the basis for Paul's confidence in a difficult missionary territory (verse 10)? In what way can this provide a model for us?
    B. Describe Paul's predicament outlined in verses 12 through 16. How does verse 17 put the capstone on this righteous reversal? How was it related to the Lord's promise of verses 9 and 10?

8

Sometimes Fast,
Sometimes Slow,
His Answers Come
to Those Below

One reason our faith can sometimes feel stranger than fiction is that God doesn't always respond to it in the same way.

Suppose that one day you look out your picture window to see a huge grass fire racing toward your home. You say a quick prayer for God to deliver you and your family — and immediately the skies pour down sheets of cold rain, halting the blaze in its tracks. In joy and gratitude you run out into your front yard, loudly praising God for hearing your prayer and honoring your faith. Then you notice a small, charred lump of something in the distance. It seems to be moving. When you investigate, you discover it's Bruno, your much-loved family dog. You pray again, asking God to heal your devoted pet. You scoop up Bruno in your arms and rush him to the vet. The doctor gently examines your injured dog and, after a long time, tells you that he thinks Bruno will live — but that it will take many months for him to recover, and he'll never be "as good as new."

Now, doesn't that seem strange?

I mean, you prayed to the same God in both instances. You prayed with the same "amount" of faith — maybe with even a little more in Bruno's case, since you had just seen God act in such a powerful and miraculous way. And yet the first time the Lord moved like lightning, and the second it seemed more like molasses.

Strange! And yet that's often exactly how He operates.

Light Speed Theology

We naturally like it best when God acts quickly and decisively, like a champion roper at the rodeo. No sooner does the angry bull burst from the devil's holding pen than God ropes it, hog-ties it, and leaves it squirming on the arena floor, to the furious applause of a delighted audience. We delight in seeing God work *fast*.

And very often, that's just what He does.

I had been discipling a young man for about a year when he approached me with a thorny problem. My friend hadn't become a Christian until a few years after college graduation, and while in school he immersed himself in drinking, experimenting with drugs, and casual sex. One of his illicit sexual liaisons produced an unwanted pregnancy. With no interest in marriage, he arranged to pay for an abortion. The "romance" soured and the pair broke up. Both parties went their separate ways, and not as friends.

Years later, once he began living to please God, my friend became convinced he should somehow get in touch with this former girlfriend, ask her forgiveness, and explain that he had become a Christian. But several problems stood in the way. First, he had no idea where the girl lived; they had no contact since the breakup. Second, as a married man he worried that if he tried to communicate with the girl, she might think he wanted to renew their affair. Third, he feared that he might reopen some painful sores that would be excruciating to close. But he insisted on doing *something*; he felt God prompting him to take action.

But what?

"Steve," he said to me, "you've been a Christian for a long time. What do *you* think I should do?"

I freely admit I had no clue what to tell my friend. But I did come up with what I thought was sage, well-reasoned advice. "Boy, this is out of my league," I said, shaking my head.

"But I'll tell you what. The pastor is out of town right now, but he's due back in about five days. Why don't you give him a call, set up an appointment, and ask him? He's probably dealt with cases like this before. He'd know a lot better than I would about what you should do."

My, oh my. In one simple speech I had been humble, I had commended my pastor, and I had been wise.

Ha!

It never entered my mind what God would do next in response to the faith of one of His newest children. The following day I got a phone call from my excited friend.

"Steve, you'll never guess what happened," he said.

"You're right," I replied, "What's up?"

"My wife and I were sitting at home yesterday afternoon and the phone rang. Guess who it was?"

"I have no idea."

"It was my old girlfriend — the one I got pregnant! She just called from out of the blue — no particular reason, no agenda. I yelled to my wife and we both got on the phone. I told her I had become a Christian and asked her to forgive me for what we had done. She did. We talked for a few minutes and then she hung up. What do you think of that?"

If only he knew. I laughed at the wonder and unpredictability of the plan of God.

I thought I had been wise in suggesting that my friend wait for several days before doing anything. Meanwhile, God put on His Nikes and tore up the track, accomplishing in a moment what I never could have imagined.

That's the way it is sometimes. You're in the soup, the burner's about to be turned up to "high" — and suddenly you're not in the soup, you're eating it. And loving every moment of the whole delicious meal.

faster than a speeding bullet

One sunny day Kim Koopman was playing outside when, as children do, she decided to dash across the street. She forgot her parents' stern warnings to look both ways before leaving the sidewalk and instead bolted out into the middle of the road, heedless of traffic.

From inside the house, her mother, Beth, saw the terrible scene unfold: her daughter dashing into the street directly in the path of an oncoming car; the vehicle unable to stop. In an instant, Beth's broken heart told her the truth. Her 30-pound daughter could not win a contest with a 2,000-pound car moving at 25 miles per hour.

Beth couldn't look. She turned away in a flood of tears.

Seconds later a neighbor burst into the house, weeping that she had seen the whole thing. "I'm sorry, I'm so sorry," she cried.

Just then Beth looked up . . . and *saw her daughter standing in one piece on the other side of the road.* Impossible! There hadn't been enough time for her even to lurch back to her starting place, much less beat the car and run to the other side.

And yet, there she stood. Without a scratch.

The neighbor's jaw dropped open. And the driver swore he heard the thump of an impact. Both thought they saw the girl get hit. At first Beth could not imagine what had happened, but later concluded there could be but one answer: Psalm 91:11-12:

> For he will command his angels concerning you to guard you in all your ways; they will lift you up in their hands, so that you will not strike your foot against a stone.

Or against a bumper, apparently. Angelic intervention seemed to be the only explanation for what transpired; nothing else fit. Kim could not *possibly* have ended up where she did, yet there she was. And nobody saw how she got there — even eyewitnesses thought they saw something else.

Not only did the Lord keep Kim from physical harm, but her divine rescue immeasurably increased my friends' faith in the goodness and providence of God. In an instant and in His inimitable way, the Lord transformed a tragedy into a celebration.

slow Answers

While we prefer instantaneous responses to our faith, we have to admit that God doesn't always answer in a flash. Yet even His "slow" answers honor our faith.

Back in 1986 an aged man walked painfully to the front of Western Seminary's chapel, took a seat, and in a thick accent heavy with emotion began to recount story after story of God's providence in the midst of unspeakable horror.

"My very, very dear children," he began, "I know you are at an age when you don't like to be called children. But I call you children, not in order to demean you, but because in a very real sense of the word, you *are* my children. . . . I prayed for you, when you were babes. When we were in Communist jails, in cells 30 feet beneath the earth . . . every night, other prisoners and I would kneel and would pray for America, for its churches, and for its children. . . . You are children of the persecuted church which prayed for America."

Richard Wurmbrand, the Romanian pastor who authored *Tortured for Christ,* held us spellbound for almost an hour. He apologized for having to sit while speaking to us, but explained that 14 years of beatings had taken their toll on his feet. He could no longer stand in place for more than a few moments.

He told how he and his comrades had languished — forgotten, they thought — in gray, underground cells illuminated by a single naked light bulb dangling from the bare ceiling. He recalled how their years of imprisonment sponged away the memory of colors, how they had forgotten the voices and sometimes the faces of loved ones, how they longed to see the carefree faces of little children.

He described the mildest of the indignities inflicted on them by their Communist torturers. "They did worse things than that," he said after we gaped in disbelief, "I will not say more."

But through all the terror, he focused on just one thing: his great, majestic God, the high and Holy One, who sustained them through the interminable years of darkness. We heard no hint of bitterness, no desire to be lifted up as an example of courageous faith. Just a simple man who loved his Savior and who hoped that, someday, his country and his captors might come to that same faith. But back in 1986, there seemed little hope of that.

I heard nothing more of Pastor Wurmbrand for several years. Once the Iron Curtain began to collapse, I learned he had been asked to return to Romania to visit his Christian countrymen. In one city a Christian bookstore had opened — the first one in memory — and he was asked if he would like to see the warehouse. He did, and was led down some stairs into a small room stuffed with books.

Wurmbrand took one look, froze in surprise, spun around, and took his wife into his arms. Then in full view of all present, this elderly saint whose battered feet require him to sit while lecturing began to dance with joy.

He recognized the warehouse. Years ago it had been his cell.

God had rewarded his faith in a stunning act of power. In the very room where torturers once abused a faithful believer, many young Christians now were receiving spiritual food. Where Satan once did his best to destroy the Church, God was building it up.

Heaven had engineered a flip-flop of gargantuan proportions . . . but took many years and countless tears to accomplish it. While God had greatly honored the faith of Wurmbrand and his fellow prisoners, He didn't do so publicly for decades.

Sometimes fast, sometimes slow, His answers come to those below. We can never know ahead of time how God might choose to respond to our faith. But we *can* know ahead of time how *we* should respond, regardless of the "strange" ways our Lord deals with us. A three-step course of action seems best:

1. Remember who you are. You are not God. You do not know the end from the beginning nor can you guess how things will ultimately turn out. Experts say that more than 90 percent of the things we worry about never happen, so leave the future where it belongs: in God's very capable hands.

2. Snuggle up against God's chest. Get as near to Him as you possibly can, and quiet your heart. You must consciously downshift, because we don't do this naturally. Remember, a weaned child does not fuss and yammer and whine as it did before it grew out of that stage. It is simply content to be near its mother — and that is how we want to be in the presence of almighty God.

3. Never give up hope. The word "hope" implies that something good awaits you in the future, ready to smother you in a king-sized grizzly bear hug. You don't know its shape or its size or even its E.T.A., but it's out there. It's always too soon to give up on God. At the proper time, God will act in the most flabbergasting ways in response to your faith.

setting the stage

Are you anxious about some excruciating situation that just doesn't seem to change? Are you worried that God seems to be moving too slowly for your tastes? If so, remember that God may *right now* be setting the stage for the answer to prayer you so desperately need. So don't give up if it takes awhile to materialize!

Whether we like it or not, God just can't be scripted. That's one big reason why faith is stranger than fiction. Sometimes our Lord acts at light speed . . . and sometimes at the speed of chilled molasses.

Strange, I know. But that doesn't make the outcome any less precious.

Insight from the Bible

One thing you can say for certain about the Father of our Lord Jesus Christ: He's no cookie-cutter God. While He never ignores the faith of even the "least" believer, there's really no telling how soon He may act on that believer's behalf. Both experience and Scripture teach us that God responds to the prayers of His faithful saints in both "fast" and "slow" modes.

And to us, that seems pretty strange.

He Likes Quick

It ought to encourage us that God seems to get just as big a kick out of acting quickly as we get in watching Him do so.

We know this is true because He openly talks about it. In Isaiah 42, for example, our Lord seems anxious to describe what He loves to do.

The passage begins with a famous description of the coming Messiah, one of several "Servant Songs" featured in Isaiah. Beginning with verse 10, the prophet shifts focus to the response appropriate to both Israel and the world. The Lord overflows with glory and so does His Messiah — so give God the praise

He deserves! Then Isaiah's vision moves to the Father and what He is about to do:

> The LORD will march out like a mighty man, like a warrior he will stir up his zeal; with a shout he will raise the battle cry and will triumph over his enemies (Isa. 42:13).

Next it's time to hear from the Holy One of Israel himself, who delights in describing His war plans on behalf of His people:

> For a long time I have kept silent, I have been quiet and held myself back. *But now, like a woman in childbirth, I cry out, I gasp and pant.* I will lay waste the mountains and hills and dry up all their vegetation; I will turn rivers into islands and dry up the pools. I will lead the blind by ways they have not known, along unfamiliar paths I will guide them; I will turn the darkness into light before them and make the rough places smooth. These are the things I will do; I will not forsake them (Isa. 42:14–16, italics mine).

What an earthshaking description of God moving in power! He transforms darkness into light. He makes the rough places smooth. He swallows up rivers and blasts mountains into plains.

Notice that all this activity happens *suddenly,* like a woman giving birth. Things had been quiet for nine months; but in the middle of the night the baby decides he's waited long enough. One caution here: Make sure you don't get caught up in the welter of images connected with a delivery room. The point is not that God hurts or that labor might take several agonizing hours. Such picturesque language is intended to convey that when God is ready to move on behalf of His people, He often does so with blinding speed: "For a long time I have kept silent, I have been quiet and held myself back. *But now. . . .*"

Isaiah often returns to this theme. Six chapters later he

shows the Lord rebuking the nation Israel for her ungodliness. God sees the need to remind His people just who they are supposed to be serving:

> I foretold the former things long ago, my mouth announced them and I made them known; then *suddenly I acted,* and they came to pass (Isa. 48:3, italics mine).

The Lord knows not only the end from the beginning, He creates both of them (as well as everything in between). He frequently acts with blinding speed and in dramatic ways to remind us that faith is stranger than fiction. As beings bound by time and space, we thrill at displays of great power compressed into tiny blips.

Perhaps that's one reason why mighty thoughts of light-speed turnabouts filled Isaiah's mind. You can't roam far in his book without bumping into some version of this idea. But I think one of my favorites appears at the end of one late chapter, shining like a diamond in the noonday sun.

Isaiah has just described a future when God would regather Israel to her land in righteousness. The chapter glows with one brilliant promise after another, painting a scene of breathtaking beauty and awesome possibilities. "The least of you will become a thousand," Isaiah enthuses, "the smallest a mighty nation." But he saves the best for last. The final sentence of Isaiah 60 could well serve as the starting gun on the race track of God's speediest acts:

> I am the LORD; in its time I will do this swiftly (Isa. 60:22).

On your marks, get set . . . oops! The race looks over already. God wins! Again!

And we win with Him.

slow doesn't mean apathetic

While it's only natural to prefer speedy rescues, the Bible makes it clear that God doesn't always respond to our faith so quickly. Often He takes longer than that. Sometimes, a lot longer.

When God, through the apostle Peter, says that "with the Lord a day is like a thousand years, and a thousand years are like a day" (2 Pet. 3:8), He's reminding us that His Daytimer looks markedly different from our own. We hate that we have to wait three minutes for microwave popcorn; He seems content to spend decades in conforming us to the image of Christ. His "slowness" in working out the details of our lives — even in delivering us from some terrible problem — doesn't mean He despises our faith. It just might mean His Daytimer lies open to five years from now, while we're focused on tomorrow.

Scores of biblical examples prove the point. God promised aged Abraham a son — and then made him wait a quarter of a century before He gave him one. He allowed Israel to spend more than four hundred years in Egyptian captivity before He brought about one of the greatest rescues of all time. Jesus told us He would return to set this world aright — and we've been waiting two thousand years to see it happen.

The fact is, God sometimes acts s-l-o-w-l-y in response to our faith. He may take weeks, months, years, decades, centuries, even millennia to accomplish His purposes in us.

And that's why faith can often seem far stranger than fiction.

Perhaps one of the best biblical examples of this is the life of King David. Or perhaps I should say, David who *eventually* became king. You'll see the significance of the distinction in a moment.

We first meet David in 1 Samuel 16. Saul, the first king of Israel, had just committed the terrible sin that caused the prophet Samuel to thunder, "Because you have rejected the word of the LORD, he has rejected you as king" (1 Sam. 15:23). God then sent Samuel to Bethlehem to choose another king to rule the nation. Samuel arrives at the household of Jesse and is introduced to seven of Jesse's sons, but the Lord has chosen none of them.

> So he asked Jesse, "Are these all the sons you have?" "There is still the youngest," Jesse answered, "but he is tending the sheep." Samuel said, "Send for

him; we will not sit down until he arrives." So he sent and had him brought in. He was ruddy, with a fine appearance and handsome features. Then the LORD said, "Rise and anoint him; he is the one." So Samuel took the horn of oil and anointed him in the presence of his brothers, and from that day on the Spirit of the LORD came upon David in power (1 Sam. 16:10–13).

Note carefully David's circumstances. He is the youngest of eight boys, a young teen at most. His father did not think it necessary to schedule him for an interview with the prophet. David comes in from the fields, stinking of sheep . . . and God says, "Rise and anoint him; he is the one."

What a dramatic, divine response to a young man's faith! From neglected, smelly little brother, to king, in one swift reversal.

Or . . . maybe not so swift.

True, one of the nation's all-time greatest prophets anointed David king of Israel. But this shepherd's head wouldn't feel the weight of a crown for ages. In fact, before David finally sat on the throne, he'd be called upon to enjoy a few life experiences:

- He survived at least nine murder attempts by Saul.

- He fled for his life and feigned insanity to stay alive.

- He lived as an outlaw in caves and became an attraction for "all those who were in distress or in debt or discontented" (1 Sam. 22:2).

- He twice spared Saul's life when he could have killed him.

- He married several women and fathered many children.

- He became an expert raider and a deadly guerrilla fighter.

At long last, David became king — but only of Judah (2 Sam. 2:4). Saul's son Ish-Bosheth still ruled Israel. A war broke out between David's supporters and those of Ish-Bosheth, and

Scripture says, "The war between the house of Saul and the house of David lasted a long time" (2 Sam. 3:1). It wasn't until David reached his 30th birthday that hostilities ceased and he became the king he was anointed to be (2 Sam. 5:3–4).

When David at last sat on the throne of a unified Israel, God had finally fulfilled His word to His choice servant. *But He did it in His own time.*

Hope for the Future

It may be that you desperately need the Lord to hear and answer some specific prayer. You feel that if your circumstances don't change soon, all hope is lost.

At a weekend retreat I spoke to a young man who felt exactly this way. He couldn't understand why God seemed to have placed his life "on hold."

So what should you do if you find yourself in a divine holding pattern? If you feel caught in a long struggle between the forces of light and the forces of darkness, what *can* you do?

There's probably no one better to ask than David himself. He wrote the following potent prescription in Psalm 131:

> My heart is not proud, O LORD, my eyes are not haughty; I do not concern myself with great matters or things too wonderful for me. But I have stilled and quieted my soul; like a weaned child with its mother, like a weaned child is my soul within me. O Israel, put your hope in the LORD both now and forevermore (Ps. 131:1–3).

Rest in His arms, child of God. Rest there; trust there; hope there. Whether the answer you need comes quickly or over time, it will come.

Hasn't your Lord promised?

Questions for Further Study

1. Read Isaiah 40:21–24.
    A. What picture of God is painted in verses 21 through 23? If you had to choose one word to describe this pic-

ture, what would it be? What bearing on swift divine action does this passage have?

B. How does verse 24 picture a swift divine response to faith? Who is involved? What significance does this hold for you?

2. Read Luke 4:23–30.

A. Describe the situation in this passage. Who is involved? What is the danger?

B. In what way does verse 30 describe a swift divine intervention? Why was a swift intervention required?

3. Read Psalm 13.

A. Have you ever felt like the Psalmist in this passage? If so, describe your situation.

B. How can you tell the Psalmist wishes to believe in "slow" or "delayed" divine interventions? How does he help himself to move toward this goal (verses 5–6)? Would this practice help you? Why or why not?

4. Read 2 Peter 3:3–9.

A. Do the people described in verses 3 and 4 believe God sometimes responds in a "slow" way to their faith? How does their belief (or unbelief) translate into action?

B. How does Peter respond to these people in verses 5 through 7? What examples does he cite? How does he use these examples to show the way in which God sometimes responds "slowly" to faith?

C. Does God ever act "slowly" from His viewpoint (verses 8–9)? How can these verses help us to wait patiently when it becomes necessary?

9

At the Last Moment

If anyone knows about real drama, it's God. Think about it. The kind of plays and movies that really get our blood pumping are the ones in which the hero falls into some terrible danger, the sky grows black as night, and it looks as if evil has triumphed over good — except at the last possible moment, some unexpected turn reverses everything. Good wins after all!

While I doubt whether God spends much time pondering popular movies and plays, I do know that He pioneered last-moment rescues. The Bible bursts with them — and so do the lives of His children.

Never Before the Time

In his long and faithful ministry of more than 60 years, Alexander Maclaren often saw God's fondness for acting at the last moment in response to the faith of His people. In one sermon based on the life of Abraham, this "prince of expository preachers" drew a stirring picture for his congregation of an aged man about to take the life of the son he loved. Abraham had prayed for Isaac to be born, and the miracle birth took place just as God promised it would (even though both Abraham and his wife, Sarah, were well past the age of childbearing). And yet, for some strange reason, God instructed Abraham to take Isaac to the top of Mt. Moriah and there sacrifice this beloved son of promise. With his heart breaking, Abraham, in faith, did as he was told.

And that's when God stepped in at the last moment, as Maclaren explained:

> Remember, only when Abraham stands with knife in hand, expecting that the next moment it will run red with his son's blood — only then does the call come: "Abraham!" Only then does he notice the ram caught in the thicket.
>
> That is God's way always. Up to the very edge we are driven, before He puts out His hand to help us. It is best for us that we should be brought to desperation, to say, "My foot slips" and then, just as our toes feel the ice, help comes and His mercy holds us up. At the last moment — never before it, never until we have discovered how much we need it, and never too late — comes the Helper.[1]

Why does God so often wait until the last moment to step in and rescue His endangered sons and daughters? Why does He seem to love such dramatic, show-stopping displays of divine power?

For one thing, He's out to build our faith, and we are the sort of people who tend to respond strongly to middle-of-the-night rescues. And for another thing — well, faith is stranger than fiction, and last-moment divine deliveries fit that description to a T.

salvation in the solomons

A few years ago some young field evangelists with Every Home for Christ not only witnessed one of God's last-moment rescues, they lived it. Their faith-building experience took place in the mountain district of the Solomon Islands in the Coral Sea, not far from Australia.

The missionaries decided to venture into the territory of the 20,000-member Koio tribe, even though tribe members had earlier murdered a British government official and three Catholic priests. After spending a week praying and fasting, the EHFC workers approached a Koio village. Immediately warriors seized them and brought them before six tribal elders who sat outside the quarters of their gravely ill high chief. The workers quickly saw that they would never be permitted to share the gospel with the Koio people without the chief's blessing — but how could he give such a blessing from the grave? Knowing that God knew better what to do than they did, they prayed that their Lord would intervene.

Did He ever — but not in the way any of them had expected.

To the workers' delight, tribal leaders suddenly decided to permit the missionaries to meet their chief and speak with him. Team members eagerly followed a guide into the chief's private bedroom and soon came face to face with a frail old man lying in a traditional "earth bed," a hollow dug out of the ground. To their astonishment, the chief not only gave the missionaries his full attention, but recited a prayer asking the Lord Jesus to become his Savior.

Here was the opening they had prayed for! Or was it? As soon as the chief finished his prayer, *he quit breathing and slumped to the ground, dead.*

It's important to remember here that a last-moment divine rescue requires that the skies must first turn dark and threatening. In this case, the heavens opened and a monsoon poured down.

As soon as the villagers realized what had happened, their interest in the newcomers turned from curiosity to fury. These white men had not healed their chief, but killed him! Furious with rage, the villagers turned on their visitors. Now the evangelists prayed as never before. If ever they needed God to act at the last moment, it was now.

The moment came.

With the lives of the young evangelists hanging in the balance, a second miracle occurred. The old chief suddenly revived and sat straight up in bed. The villagers were awestruck when he called for 60 close friends and family members to gather for a special meeting. As they crowded around him, the old man related a vivid account of what he had seen in the previous hours — an amazing story of heaven and hell, angels and Jesus.

"I have returned," the chief told his astonished people, "to tell you that we must stop worshiping false gods, and that we must listen to the message these men have brought to our village." After admonishing the workers to continue their witness, the Koio's chief quietly passed away for good.[2]

The chief returned to this world for only two hours, but it was long enough for God to honor the faith of His servants with a remarkable last-moment rescue. Maclaren got it exactly right: "At the last moment — never before it, never until we have discovered how much we need it, and never too late — comes the Helper."

Within minutes of their leader's death, all six village elders made commitments to Christ. As news of the incident spread throughout the Koio's territory, nine churches and 36 smaller fellowships quickly were established — all in an area without any gospel witness prior to mid-1990. Within a few years, almost four thousand Koios professed faith in Christ, including a group of three hundred believers from the deceased chief's village.

What novelist could have dreamed up such a story? None but God. Our Lord loves to prove through His last-moment rescues that faith really is stranger than fiction.

not so fast

We may not always understand God's sense of timing, but that doesn't take away from its exquisite nature. "Up to the very edge we are driven, before He puts out His hand to help us," says Maclaren, and I think he's right. I think he's also right about why God so often operates this way in response to our faith: "It is best for us that we should be brought to desperation, to say, 'My foot slips' and then, just as our toes feel the ice, help comes and His mercy holds us up."

I experienced this firsthand when I moved from the Midwest to Oregon. After finishing two emotionally tough years at grad school, I took a year off to regain balance and perspective. At the end of that time I decided to finish my degree at another school in San Diego. A friend of mine, Bruce DeRoos, found out I was planning to head over to the West Coast, and he asked if I might be willing to change my plans a bit and drive with him to Portland. I could spend a couple of weeks in the Pacific Northwest — a new adventure — and then I could work my way down to Southern California.

Sounded like a plan to me, so I jumped at it.

When we left Wisconsin on January 8, the thermometer read 12 degrees and three feet of snow covered the ground. I felt more than ready to leave.

Four days later when we drove into Portland on Interstate 84, we marveled at the way the sun's bright rays reflected off of the Columbia River, illuminating the sheer basalt cliff walls of the Gorge. It took away our breath — and so did the 70-degree temperature that greeted us.

Hmmmm, I thought. *Maybe I don't need San Diego.* (At the time I didn't know that January in Oregon doesn't usually look like this . . . but that's another story.)

Bruce and I soon settled into an apartment, and I made an appointment to visit Western Seminary on the east side of the city. I had heard good things about the school and wanted to drop in on a class. One visit to professor Jim Andrews' classroom convinced me that I ought to finish my degree at Western. Only one problem remained, and it didn't seem like a big one: I needed a part-time job.

Immediately I started praying to find employment. I checked the *Oregonian* classifieds every day and felt sure I'd quickly find just the right position. I'd never had trouble finding work, and I didn't expect any problems this time around.

But days turned into weeks and weeks into months, and still I couldn't find a job. Convenience stores didn't want to hire someone with a college degree, and a few promising interviews ended up promising more than they delivered. By this time Bruce had returned to Wisconsin for lack of funds, and it looked as if I might have to follow suit.

I felt like a failure and I couldn't understand what God was doing (or not doing). Western looked like the perfect school — didn't the Lord want me there? I'd spent months looking for a suitable part-time job, and now my money had nearly run out. I could stick around only a few more days, then would have to tuck my tail between my legs and retreat 2,000 miles to the east.

I described my predicament to Pat Edmonds, a good friend from my home church who moved out to Oregon a year before I did, and he said he'd enlist the prayers of his colleagues at a youth outreach ministry. As I started making plans to pack, Pat told my story to his friends — and that night one of them said he might have a job lead for me. He arranged for me to interview with Fae Brown at Multnomah Press, and a day or so later I found myself in her office, accepting a position as a telephone marketer.

I didn't need to pack after all! God moved at the last moment to keep me in Oregon and allow me to enroll me at Western.

It soon turned out that I stank as a telephone marketer (I lasted a week and a half), but God had already arranged for me to spend a few months in MP's warehouse, shipping Christian books all over the world. I began praying about using my journalism skills in book publishing, a year later I became an editor, and that's been my primary occupation ever since.

Now, here's the question: If God knew all along that He wanted me in the Christian book industry, why didn't He just send me in that direction to begin with? Why make me wait until the last moment, then send me to a job that I hated (and badly botched), and only after several months had passed, open the door to a life path that I absolutely love (even though it had never before occurred to me)?

I think that by now you know the answer to that question: Faith is stranger than fiction! And God's last-moment rescues somehow build our faith as almost nothing else can.

oops! into wow!

Many last-moment rescues seem more hilarious than dramatic. Author Rebecca Manley Pippert knows all about that. In her excellent book on friendship evangelism, *Out of the Saltshaker and into the World,* Becky tells of an encounter she had with Lois — bright, sensitive, and skeptical about the existence of God.[3] After several conversations, Becky invited Lois to a Bible study in a dorm room at Stanford University. "Okay, I'll come," Lois responded. "But the Bible won't have anything relevant to say to me."

The next day Becky discovered Lois was living off campus with her boyfriend, Phil. He decided to join her at the study. Without knowing Lois's background, Becky chose John 4 as the study text, a passage about a woman with multiple sexual partners. It was then that Becky began to sweat:

> I began introducing the chapter to the group, noticed Phil and Lois sitting there, and suddenly remembered the passage dealt with a woman who had sexual problems. I feared Lois would think I had planned this just for her.
>
> With a step of faith, I frantically tried to think of how to avoid the crunch of the passage (though I was sure God had got me into this mess). Lois and Phil were seated close to my left. Thinking it would be better if Lois did not read the passage aloud, I called on Sally, who was immediately to my right, calculating that if each person read a paragraph aloud, we would finish before it was Lois's turn.
>
> To my dismay a girl three seats away from Lois started reading. (I discovered later it was Sally's twin sister who happened to be sitting next to me.) Then Lois read the portion: "Jesus said to her, 'You are right in saying, "I have no husband". . . for the man you're living with now is not your husband.' " It was her first experience of reading Scripture and her eyes grew as big as saucers, while I hid behind my Bible!
>
> "I must say, this is a bit more relevant than I had expected," she commented with considerable understatement.

This comical last-moment intervention began with an outmaneuvered Bible study leader and would conclude the next day when Lois saw the truth of the gospel and committed her life to Christ. Or did it really conclude then? Perhaps not. Lois immediately moved out of her apartment with Phil, a choice which infuriated him (but prompted three other girls to get right with Jesus). The next day school officials told Lois she could move into a dorm — unheard of at such a late date — and her roommate turned out to be a dynamic, mature Christian. "Wow, what an intervention!" you say. Yes, but it still wasn't over. Three months later Phil became a Christian. After his conversion he told his former lover, "Thanks, Lois, for loving God enough to put Him first instead of me. Your obedience affected my eternal destiny."

Ah, the sweet exhilaration of serving a God who delights in honoring the faith of His children with full-throttle, last-moment rescues! At just the right time — and not a moment before — He zips in and exchanges gloom for glory.

Just where He wants us

I know that God's last-moment rescues tend to fray our nerves, but they also tend to build our faith. And that's the point, isn't it? No doubt it would make our lives more comfortable and less unpredictable if God didn't have such a passion for entering the big scene just before the curtain drops. But as the Master Playwright, He knows best how to keep the actors on their toes . . . and the audience on its feet.

And that's just where He wants us.

Insight from the Bible

If you're looking for biblical patterns to help you grasp how God responds to the faith of His people, it's good to remember that He himself told us He's coming "in a flash, in the twinkling of an eye, at the last trumpet" (1 Cor. 15:52).

Look for Him at the *last* trump, not the *first*.

Throughout biblical history, God has demonstrated a fondness for waiting until the very last moment before He moves in power to rescue His believing children. Of course, He doesn't always do it this way, but He does it enough that we ought to be prepared to see His last-moment wonders in our own lives.

The pattern starts early

Even at the very beginning, we see God's inclination toward last-moment activity.

Before sin ever entered our world, before the air rang with the sound of a baby's cry, before the first weed sprouted or the first thorn pierced a finger, God was busy preparing a last-moment blessing for Adam . . . a blessing named Eve.

Have you ever wondered why God paraded all the animals before Adam, asking him to name each one, before He ever got around to making Eve? Why not create both man and woman at the same time, out of the same lump of clay, and then allow them as a team to think of names like giraffe and caribou and musk oxen? Why wait until the "last moment" to reveal Adam's true partner?

Or jump ahead to the days of Noah, when the Lord called forth a great flood to wipe sinful mankind from the face of the earth. We don't know how long it took Noah to build his enormous ship, but no one constructs a vessel 450 feet long, 75 feet wide, and 45 feet high in a few days. During the whole time the ark was taking shape, Peter implies that Noah was preaching to his doomed neighbors (2 Pet. 2:5). No one listened.

Finally, after Noah finished his ark and all its animal cargo had walked or flown or slithered aboard, Noah and his family also entered their soon-to-be-floating home. At that precise moment, God himself shut the door of the ark, broke open all the "springs of the great deep," and opened "the floodgates of heaven" (Gen. 7:11–16).

Now, couldn't the Lord have sent a few raindrops before opening heaven's floodgates, just as a warning shot? Before the rains fell, couldn't He have shown Noah's family that their dear old dad hadn't really flipped his lid? Why wait until the last moment?

But maybe the most powerful early example of God's delight in last-moment action is an unforgettable incident in the life of Abraham, the man the apostle Paul calls "the man of faith" (Gal. 3:9).

A severe test of faith

Genesis 12 tells how God called Abraham out of Ur of the Chaldeans to go and settle in Canaan, the land of promise. At the same time the Lord told Abraham that He would make him into a "great nation" and He would give the Promised Land to his "offspring." It was quite a pledge, for Abraham and his wife, Sarah, had no children.

Many years went by, and still Abraham and Sarah produced no heirs. Sarah had long since passed the age of childbearing, and Abraham, at nearly 100 years of age, looked "as good as dead" (Rom. 4:19). So naturally God chose that unlikely moment to announce that He was about to fulfill His promise — and Abraham believed Him.

Nine months later, little Isaac arrived on the scene.

Abraham loved his son and raised him in the fear of the Lord. But one day that very Lord came to Abraham with a fearful command. He told this aged man to "take your son, your only son, Isaac, whom you love," and sacrifice him atop Mt. Moriah (Gen. 22:2). Incredibly, Abraham obeyed. He told his son (who was probably a teenager by then) only that they would offer a sacrifice to the Lord; he did not tell him that Isaac himself was to be the sacrifice. When Isaac asked, "Father? The fire and wood are here, but where is the lamb for the burnt offering?" Abraham replied, "God himself will provide the lamb for the burnt offering, my son" (Gen. 22:7–8).

This elderly man of faith then built an altar, bound his son with ropes, placed him on the firewood, and raised a knife-wielding hand to strike dead the son he so deeply loved.

Only then — at the very last moment — did God stop His servant from taking Isaac's life. An angel of the Lord called out, "Abraham! Abraham! Do not lay a hand on the boy. Do not do anything to him. Now I know that you fear God, because you have not withheld from me your son, your only son" (Gen. 22:12).

As soon as Abraham looked up (I'm sure, through tears), he saw a ram caught by its horns in a thicket. With great joy he took the animal and sacrificed it instead of his boy. The passage concludes, "So Abraham called that place The LORD Will Provide. And to this day it is said, 'On the mountain of the LORD it will be provided' " (Gen. 22:14).

To this day we, too, can say that the Lord will provide. But just as in Abraham's case, we find that He sometimes provides at the very last moment — as the buzzer sounds, with no time left on the clock.

That's one reason why we can confidently say, faith is stranger than fiction.

The pattern continues

The New Testament continues this pattern of last-moment divine intervention in response to the faith of God's people.

We see it right away in the narrative of Jesus' birth. In the very first chapter of Matthew, Joseph learns that his betrothed is pregnant — and he knows he isn't the father. Just before he divorces Mary, God sends an angel to tell him to go ahead with the marriage, for Mary carries the very Son of God. So far, so good. But why didn't God just tell Joseph beforehand what He was about to do? That's exactly what He did for Mary (Luke 1:26–38). Why let Joseph stew until the last moment? I'm not sure. But that's what God did.

Or consider what happened after the Magi visited the holy family. These wise men from the East came to honor Jesus, the King of the Jews (who was then probably about two years old), while the wicked King Herod wanted Him dead. Herod instructed the Magi to return after their visit, so that he, too, could honor the newborn king. When they failed to return, he sent his vicious troops to the sleepy little village of Bethlehem to slaughter all the boys two years old and younger. In the middle of the previous night, God warned Joseph in a dream to take his family to Egypt and flee the coming carnage. Now, God knew all along how Herod would react; Matthew even includes an ancient prophecy from Jeremiah 31:15 to that effect. Yet the Lord waited until the last moment to warn Joseph to get up and leave. Why?

Or consider yet another famous episode from the earthly ministry of Jesus. Everyone knew that Jesus loved Lazarus and considered him one of His best friends. So when Lazarus fell deathly ill, his sisters expected that Jesus would come running. Yet John says when Jesus "heard that Lazarus was sick, he stayed where he was two more days" (John 11:6). Shortly afterward, Lazarus died.

Now, I ask you: Is that any "normal" way to treat a close friend? Isn't there something just a little strange about it?

The dead man's sisters certainly thought it seemed an odd

way to act. Both Mary and Martha told Jesus, with hurt in their voices, "If you had been here, my brother would not have died" (John 11:21, 32).

Jesus, however, had acted deliberately. He even told His disciples, "Lazarus is dead, and for your sake I am glad I was not there, so that you may believe" (John 11:14–15). At the heart of Christ's "strange" response lies an overwhelming desire for something far greater than human comfort or peace of mind. At the white-hot center of His actions is a passionate longing that His followers "believe" — even if He causes them tremendous emotional pain in the process.

Do we really think it will be any different for us than it was for Mary and Martha? Do we really believe that Jesus will refuse to go to great lengths to build our faith? Do we really imagine that He will shrink from applying pain if that's what it takes to do the work?

Our Lord loves last-moment rescues — even if they cause us to tremble, even if we think the "last moment" has already passed — because He knows they will build our faith and glorify His name. Remember, at the beginning of this episode with Lazarus, Jesus told His followers, "This sickness will not end in death. No, it is for God's glory so that God's Son may be glorified through it" (John 11:4).

And that, of course, is just how it turned out. Lazarus' sickness did not "end" in death (even though death was allowed to reign for a few days), for Jesus raised His friend back to life. The Master stepped in at the last moment to display His glory and to honor the faith of His loved ones. And the result? "Many of the Jews who had come to visit Mary, and had seen what Jesus did, put their faith in him" (John 11:45).

Faith is stranger than fiction — especially in last-moment rescues that, for a little while, seem just a little too late.

The Discipline of waiting

It's always too early to give up on a God who relishes buzzer-beating finishes. It's never the right time to abandon hope when you serve a loving Lord who loves to act at the "last moment."

The prophet Isaiah proclaimed this very message to his weary countrymen who longed for God to do for them what

He had done for their forefathers. Isaiah gave voice to their yearnings when he wrote:

> Oh, that you would rend the heavens and come down, that the mountains would tremble before you! As when fire sets twigs ablaze and causes water to boil, come down to make your name known to your enemies and cause the nations to quake before you! For when you did awesome things that we did not expect, you came down, and the mountains trembled before you (Isa. 64:1–3).

Isaiah remembers a time when God acted in power for the benefit of His faithful people, and he pleads that his Lord would so act again. He recalls how the might of heaven once shook mountains and scorched the countryside and terrified Israel's enemies . . . and he wants those good times to roll again.

Do you ever feel like that? Do you ever wish that God would repeat some miracle or last-moment intervention that blessed you in the past? There's nothing wrong with expressing such a wish, as long as we don't *demand* that God stretch out His hand for us in exactly the same way as He did before.

In any event, rarely do we know when the actual "last moment" has arrived. It always *feels* like the last moment to us — which is exactly why God tells us to trust Him. Isaiah gives us precisely the right word for those times when we feel as if we just can't wait any longer for God to act. The prophet tells us:

> Since ancient times, no one has heard, no ear has perceived, no eye has seen any God beside you, who acts on behalf of those who wait for him (Isa. 64:4).

For whom does God promise to act? For those who take matters into their own hands? For those who fret? For those who scheme? No. God promises to act *only* on behalf of those who *wait* for Him.

The apostle Paul paraphrases this verse in 1 Corinthians 2:9 where he writes, "No eye has seen, no ear has heard, no mind has conceived what God has prepared for those who love him." Don't miss a couple of significant changes the Apostle makes.

First, Paul changes the phrase, "who *acts*" (present tense) to "what God *has prepared*" (past perfect tense). In the apostle's mind, it is so certain that God will act on behalf of His people, that we can consider His actions to be *already accomplished*. In other words, as you read these words, God has in store for you precisely the right remedy for your problem. He doesn't have to think about what to do; He's already done it. It has only to be revealed.

Second, Paul changes the phrase "on behalf of those who wait for him," to "for those who love him." Through this remarkable switch, Paul connects love with waiting. Those who wait for God to act on their behalf demonstrate their love for the Lord; those who refuse to wait demonstrate their lack of love.

In other words, there's not much difference between, "How much do I love God?" and "How long am I willing to wait for God?"

why should i wait Anymore?

It's *hard* to wait. I know that. Last-moment rescues may strengthen our faith in the end, but what do we do in the meanwhile?

Whatever you do, I beg you not to follow the pattern of one of ancient Israel's kings. The armies of Aram had besieged his city for a long time and his people had descended into cannibalism. As he inspected Samaria, his devastated capital, he cried out, "This disaster is from the LORD" (2 Kings 6:33).

Now, before you judge him too harshly for this statement, you should know that he was *right*. Samaria found itself in deep distress because its people had abandoned the Lord. They had gone their own way and rejected God's best plan for them. God had appointed the siege as a means of discipline and restoration. How the people responded would determine their destiny.

Although the Lord wanted His people to turn from their sin, the king displayed his unbelief when he blurted out the second half of his statement. "Why should I wait for the LORD any longer?" he asked.

Oh, if only he had read the next chapter, 2 Kings 7! Then he would have gaped in wonder at the mighty, last-moment rescue God had waiting, just around the corner.

That very evening, the Lord placed in the ears of the invaders the sounds of an (imaginary) attacking force infinitely stronger than themselves. The enemy soldiers ran in panic clear back to Aram, abandoning all their provisions, their animals, their lodging, even their weapons.

The next morning, the starving city feasted on the bounty of its enemies — all except for one of the king's officers, who had responded to God's prediction of the rescue by scoffing, "Look, even if the LORD should open the floodgates of the heavens, could this happen?" (2 Kings 7:2). The next morning the starving inhabitants of Samaria trampled that officer when they rushed out to fill their bloated bellies — just as foretold.

Come to think of it, both the king *and* the officer could have benefited from reading 2 Kings 7.

But, of course, that was impossible, since the text hadn't yet been written. No, to participate joyfully in God's amazing last-moment rescue, they would simply have to live by faith . . . *just like you and me!*

I can't point to any earthly book that details exactly how God will respond to your faith or mine. But 2 Kings 7 does teach us that those who wait in faith get fed; those who scoff get trampled.

So I plead with you, don't be like the king. Don't follow the example of his officer. The only safe and wise course of action is to wait in faith for God.

Don't *give* up! *Look* up! Who knows? You may be just around the corner from a last-moment rescue of your own.

questions for further study

1. Read Exodus 14:1–31.

    A. Describe the predicament that befell Israel in this passage.

    B. Notice that God specifically instructed the Israelites to "turn back" into a camp that made no strategic military sense. Why would He do such a thing?

C. How did God deliver His people at the last moment? Why do you think He waited until the last moment?

2. Read 2 Chronicles 32:1–23.
   A. Describe the predicament that befell Judah in this passage.
   B. Notice that this predicament befell Judah, not after great sin, but "after all that Hezekiah had so faithfully done" (verse 1). Why do you think God often allows severe trials into our lives after we have been faithful to Him?
   C. How did God deliver His people at the last moment? Why do you think He waited until the last moment?

3. Read Galatians 6:9.
   A. What kinds of things prompt us to "become weary in doing good"? How does God's timing sometimes tempt us to become weary?
   B. What promise is given in this verse? How can we disqualify ourselves from receiving this promise?
   C. In regard to this verse, why would it be wise for us to remember God's fondness for last-moment rescues?

10

The Agony of Victory

Have you ever met someone with a Pollyanna outlook? He or she refuses to acknowledge the sorrows or difficulties of real life. Such a misguided believer might greet a diagnosis of cancer with a glassy-eyed "Praise the Lord," or respond to the death of a beloved child with a soul-deadening, "Rejoice; again I say, rejoice."

From my perspective, the problem with the Pollyannas of the world is that they don't seem familiar with this one. We all ought to look for the bright side, but only a lunatic calibrates his sundial at midnight.

God never asked us to pretend that evil does not exist, that pain is illusory, and that everything you've always hoped for will be delivered to your door come sunrise. Life on this fallen planet just isn't like that.

Only a couple of days ago a good friend told me that a cheery little 12-year-old boy from his church drowned over the weekend. The boy had been playing with his friends, each one trying to outdistance the other in contests of underwater swimming. At one point the boy said he felt a little dizzy, but then everyone went back to playing. Before long his friends noticed him motionless at the bottom of the pool. At first they thought he was fooling around, but when one lad grabbed his friend's arm and found it limp, they all knew something had gone terribly wrong. By the time they got him to the surface, his lips had turned blue and not even immediate CPR could revive him. He died at the hospital a little while later, without ever regaining consciousness.

This boy attended a solid Christian school and expressed a strong faith in Christ. At his packed-out memorial service, several of his believing buddies moved the adults to tears with heartfelt tributes to their fallen friend.

So what happened? Isn't a strong faith in God supposed to shield us from this kind of tragedy? And what would the Polyanna Christians say to this grieving family? That they didn't have enough faith? That they ought to smile and thank God for the untimely death? That things will feel better in the morning?

The hard truth is, people get hurt in this world. They betray one another. They fall ill, get in accidents, say spiteful things, lose their jobs, cheat, steal, fail exams, are evicted from their homes, and die prematurely.

Even Christian people.

In this chapter I want to make it as clear as I can that our faith doesn't disconnect us from the real world. I want to discourage anyone from concluding that their faith, however strong, exempts them from the hardships common to our sinful race and the troubles specific to believers. God honors our faith in ways that best please Him. Although it is certain our Lord will deliver His people, it is seldom clear how or when He will do so.

Second, I want to go on record that God *is* honoring His people's faith even when He refuses to spare them the slightest pain. I rejoice that God often prevents Satan's fiery darts from reaching us. But sometimes God permits those flaming arrows to find their mark, *even as He continues to honor our faith.*

Many of us find this a hard idea to accept. We have grown so used to hearing about "the thrill of victory and the agony of defeat" that we have forgotten some triumphs hurt. There is such a thing as the agony of victory.

In 1939 the author J.R.R. Tolkien coined a term to describe this idea. In a famous essay on fairy stories (remember, Tolkien wrote *The Hobbit* and *The Lord of the Rings* trilogy) he used the word *eucatastrophe* to describe a sudden turn of the story in which darkness turns into light and evil into good. But he insisted this reversal "is not essentially 'escapist' or 'fugitive.' In its fairy tale — or other-world — setting, it is a sudden and miraculous grace: never to be counted on to return." Neither did this reversal deny or make light of sorrow and failure, for their possibility "is necessary to the joy of deliverance." What he did deny was a "universal final defeat."[1]

That well describes the agony of triumph. God does not always deliver His people from great pain. Sometimes He does; at other times He doesn't. But in all cases, God honors the faith of His people in ways that prove He rules from heaven. At His word, even the worst schemes of men and devils serve to proclaim His glory.

They march in the same parade

In junior high and high school I marched in several parades as a member of the drum section. It was our job to help the band march in unison (which partially explains why it sometimes didn't). Some parades last longer than others. While short parades appeal to musicians, long ones often score more points with the audience — especially if the show looks spectacular. Floats, clowns, bands, antique cars, horses, and beauty queens (and sometimes even blimps) can make for an unforgettable parade.

The parade of saints who know the agony of victory snakes on for a long, long distance. Their parade highlights the work of a God who honors their faith in many ways . . . each response different, each act surprising, yet each one unforgettable.

Part of the parade is even now winding its way through Communist China. In one area of Henan province, a church of 260,000 believers grew to about 600,000 in less than ten years. In Szechwan province, where 1 of every 40 people on earth live, nearly two thousand new churches were planted in the first two to three years of the past decade. Even the government recognizes the nation's mushrooming interest in the gospel. A bulletin released by the Beijing Statistical Bureau stated that 75 million Christians live in China — triple the membership of the Communist Party.

Just decades ago experts thought the Church in China had all but disappeared. Now millions of Chinese are embracing Christ in an explosion of belief . . . and shrapnel is flying everywhere.

Not long ago, according to one reporter, "local Communist

authorities in some provinces began detaining, fining, and beating Christians for their religious activities. In Henan province, government officials made this decree: "It was you Christians who brought down the regimes in eastern Europe and the Soviet Union, but here in China we will stop you now!"[2]

Communist authorities made good on their threats, escalating raids on Christian meetings. Hundreds of foreign mission workers were arrested, beaten, and jailed.

The authorities tried their best to turn back the work God had already accomplished. They displayed some of their tactics in Anhui province, where devastating floods prompted believers to mount relief efforts for their brethren. Party functionaries moved quickly:

> With almost unbelievable callousness, Communist officials declared that flood victims who believe in Jesus are not to be given relief help. To the 20,000 affected Christians, the government message has been: "Tell them to go to their God for food and clothes."
>
> When Christians from Shanghai donated clothing for these fellow believers, they were promptly arrested, and their relief supplies were seized. When Anhui churches took up offerings from their own people to buy bread for both Christian and non-Christian flood victims, the government accused the believers of trying to bribe people to convert, then confiscated the food and beat those involved.[3]

Still, God continues to move in response to the faith of His persecuted people. David Wang, president of Asian Outreach, told of a woman whom authorities fined the equivalent of five years' wages for her Christian activities. When friends came to bail her out of jail, she refused: "My mission is to minister the gospel to sinners," she said. "What better place for me to be?"[4]

This woman understands the agony of victory.

curiouser and curiouser

An American woman also came to embrace the agony of victory. Doctors diagnosed Kathy with breast cancer just five days before her mom died in a car accident. Her anger flared at both her father — who fell asleep at the wheel — and at God. She confessed to a lot of bitter questioning.

About that time Kathy joined a new church and was beginning to get her relationship with God on solid ground. When she underwent surgery the August following the crash, the people of her church crowded around to help. Her pastor offered special comfort — he didn't pretend to know why God allowed both catastrophes to happen almost simultaneously, but he knew God cared.

Kathy joined a small fellowship group that began to change her thinking. She soon abandoned her childhood conviction that she must have done something sinful to deserve her troubles. In fact, she began to believe that her illness allowed her the chance to give and others to receive, for everyone to learn the nature of true community.

Several months later Kathy's back began acting up. Her co-workers urged her to see a doctor, and tests revealed she had developed yet another form of cancer, *multiple myeloma*. Her heart sank.

"I thought it was unfair that I had to get it again," she said. This time, because she had a hard time getting out of the house, she lost much of her support system.

When she entered the hospital, she heard "a lot of talk about getting my affairs in order, that I didn't have much time left." But God had other plans. "Later my oncologist said I should be thinking about years left instead of months," Kathy said.

Treatment helped strengthen Kathy's back and she stopped feeling as weak as she once did, but could anything good come out of *this?*

Yes, according to Kathy. The whole painful ordeal strengthened her relationship with God, made it more realistic. She learned that sometimes He doesn't heal our bodies, but uses the affliction to teach us — and not necessarily just the afflicted one.

"Now I stop and rely on Him to make it through every day," Kathy said, and her friends agreed. They found it remarkable that this was the same woman who used to doubt that God worked in the lives of His people or that He could really, truly, love *her*.

And what was it that made possible this remarkable spiritual growth? Cancer. Go figure.

And by the way, this story doesn't end with the traditional "happily-ever-after" ending. Kathy's illness eventually killed her — and yet God used it to honor and strengthen her faith, as well as the faith of her friends.

This story reminds us that God does not always respond to our faith with happy bells and whistles . . . and yet His loving hand remains unmistakable all the same.

Breakthrough in Balangao

Joanne Shetler, the Wycliffe missionary we met earlier, is yet another believer who is coming to understand the agony of victory. After living for years among the Balangaos, only two had put their trust in Christ. This made Shetler heartsick. On a trip back to California to visit her home church, the weary missionary poured out her heart. Even her own "father," Ama, didn't believe — he and the rest of the tribe remained too fearful of powerful evil spirits.

So Shetler's home church began praying: "God, show the Balangaos that You're stronger than the spirits. Make the Balangaos desire You; help them believe Your Word."[5]

While the church prayed, a miracle birth took place back in the Philippines among Shetler's adopted people. Andrea, one of the two Balangao believers, had prayed to be delivered from barrenness; Melisa was God's answer. But when Shetler returned to the village, she discovered Melisa had died. Villagers buried the infant the day before Shetler returned.

No, No! Shetler thought. *Something is wrong. Surely God has made a mistake. Why, God? This baby can't die — she's an answer to our prayers! Why, God? Why?*

"I was sure that any possibility of Balangaos ever believing in God had just been demolished," Shetler wrote. "What would happen to Andrea's faith?"

To Shetler's great surprise, Andrea's faith never wavered; Balangaos grow up believing that the supernatural is all powerful and not to be questioned. Still, the other villagers frightened Andrea when they suggested that because Melisa hadn't been baptized she went to hell. Shetler used the Scripture to disprove this awful idea, but the village had to be convinced. A local tradition demanded that every villager meet each night for nine days to pray memorized prayers for the soul of the deceased. Andrea asked the missionary to come and tell the people where Melisa had gone.

The Balangaos asked a million questions. *Where did the dead go? What was it like there? Who is there? Does everyone go there?* Each night they asked more questions. *Where do we go when we die? What about the Resurrection?* They grew so interested in the discussion that they insisted upon continuing their studies even after the nine days had elapsed. They began reading the newly published Gospel of Mark.

Soon Shetler saw God go to work — a victory touched with agony. Balangaos not only listened to the gospel message, they demanded to hear it. Shetler could hardly believe it:

How can one ever predict how God will bring himself glory? The heartbreaking, premature death of my friend's baby was God's avenue to answer my prayers, and the prayers of my friends back home in California.

Some time later, after Shetler witnessed a similar episode, the stunned missionary confessed, "I was dumbfounded. . . . I simply had to resign as the manager of God's glory."

Friends, the plain truth is, none of us has the qualifications to manage God's glory. None of us is wise enough, godly enough, mature enough, or even imaginative enough to predict how, when, or where God will move in power in response to the faith of His people.

Elisabeth Elliot skillfully pointed this out in *Through Gates of Splendor*. That classic book describes the events leading up to January 8, 1956, the day five young missionaries (including Elliot's husband, Jim) were speared to death while trying to bring the gospel to a savage tribe of South American Indians called the Aucas. Nearly three years after this tragedy, Elliot found herself within ten feet of one of the seven men who killed her husband. She and her three-and-a-half-year-old daughter had returned to the Aucas' territory to point these men to the Lord. And the tribe listened.

"How did this come to be?" Elliot asked. "Only God who made iron swim, who caused the sun to stand still, in whose hand is the breath of every living thing — only this God, who is our God forever and ever, could have done it." The Aucas told Elliot they considered their attack an error; they had mistaken the white men for cannibals. Elliot, however, saw it another way:

> But we know that it was no accident. God performs all things according to the counsel of His own will. The real issues at stake on January 8, 1956, were very far greater than those which immediately involved five young men and their families, or this small tribe of naked "savages."

> God is the God of human history, and He is at work continuously, mysteriously, accomplishing His eternal purposes in us, through us, for us, and in spite of us.[6]

I think that's another way of saying that faith is stranger than fiction, and that there is such a thing as the agony of victory. John Hus might well agree.

snapshot from an old parade

The saints who have marched in the agony of victory are part of a long parade, but it's also a very old one. It stretches all the way across the world and from this moment in time to the distant past. Do you recall Martin Luther from chapter 3? He was marching in this parade before God yanked him from his place to sign for a Special Delivery. To that point, Martin had been striding shoulder to shoulder with a man named John Hus. John never received a Special Delivery, however; he kept on marching to the end.

His end.

Hus lived almost exactly a century before Martin Luther. A popular preacher in his native Bohemia (roughly equivalent to the former Czechoslovakia), Hus "raised the curtain on the Reformation on the continent, adopting Wycliffe's theology and anticipating many of the 16th century reformers' key ideas."[7] Hus scathingly criticized the pope's sale of indulgences to raise cash for a 1412 crusade against the king of Naples (the pope promised full remission of sins to anyone who supported Rome) and agreed with Wycliffe that the invisible church of the elect took precedence over the institutional, hierarchical organization. Both of his positions threatened the pope's authority and put Hus on a fast track to the stake. The archbishop excommunicated Hus in 1410; Rome followed suit in 1412.

In 1414, the Council of Constance convened to heal "the Great Schism" (in which rival popes ruled from different cities), sort out the church's problems in Bohemia, and make some long-overdue reforms. The emperor Sigismund invited Hus to attend and promised him safe conduct in both directions. Despite some hesitations, Hus decided to go. But within a month, followers of Pope John XXII seized and imprisoned Hus, and on July 6, 1415, the council proclaimed him a heretic. Church officials dragged him to the outskirts of the city, chained his neck to a stake, and burned him to death.

According to *Foxe's Book of Martyrs,* Hus refused one last offer to recant, declaring, "What error should I renounce, when I know myself guilty of none? For this was the principal end and purpose of my doctrine, that I might teach all men repentance and remission of sins, according to the verity of the gospel of Jesus Christ: wherefore, with a cheerful mind and courage, I am here ready to suffer death."[8]

As the fire crackled around his body, Hus began to sing loudly to Christ. He died a martyr to the cause of Jesus and his ashes were flung into the river Rhine so the least memory of the man might be erased.

But it was not erased. In fact, Hus's bonfire ignited a flame that one hundred years later burst into full blaze in a sleepy German town called Wittenberg. Hus never saw how God planned to honor his stubborn faith, but honor it He did. John Hus marched in the Agony of Victory parade, and angels welcomed him home with a ticker-tape celebration as big as anything Martin Luther ever enjoyed.

join the parade

Two godly men; two separate destinies. Luther received a Special Delivery; Hus endured the agony of victory. Yet both well represented the Father of lights — Luther by igniting the Reformation and Hus by illuminating his countrymen with the sacrifice of himself.

The life of John Hus proves not only that faith is stranger than fiction, but also that it's far more compelling. Real life — even with all its pain, sorrow, hardships, and tears — offers wonders beyond any fairy tale.

Sorry about that, Pollyanna. (But you're always welcome to join the parade.)

insight from the Bible

Fans of the Olympics can never forget the remarkable performance turned in by Kerri Strug at the 1996 summer games. While all America held its collective breath, this diminutive gymnast summoned up her courage to complete a vault that would assure the first all-around gold medal for the U.S. Women's Gymnastics team.

While television cameras focused on her delicate-but-determined face, this fierce competitor with the high-pitched voice studied the runway, ran down it full speed, then vaulted to a 9.712 score and a smashing victory for the red, white and blue.

And she did it all on a severely sprained ankle.

Better than most athletes, Kerri Strug knows about the agony of victory. She knows that some victories hurt, and hurt badly.

And that's what makes them all the sweeter.

We need to learn the same thing if we hope to advance very far in the Christian faith. A genuine, growing faith does not excuse us from the pain that strikes everyone in this world. But it can win for us a smashing victory, even if tinged with agony.

Hot and Bothered in Babylon

Daniel 3:16–18 has always been one of my favorite Old Testament texts. The third chapter of Daniel tells the familiar story of three Hebrew captives — Shadrach, Meshach, and Abednego — who refused to worship King Nebuchad-nezzar's golden statue. For their defiance the king tossed them into a furnace heated seven times hotter than usual. Yet God spared their lives and used the incident to teach the king that even he, the greatest of all human rulers, amounted to less than a gnat in God's scheme of things. The chapter ends with a classic declaration that faith is stranger than fiction: "Then the king promoted Shadrach, Meshach and Abednego in the province of Babylon" (Dan. 3:30).

From toast to tops in one quick step!

The story has thrilled readers for millennia, but for our purposes I would like to focus on verses 16 through 18. I believe this passage offers tremendous clues on how to persevere in faith whether God spares us pain or not. There are good reasons why God's servants were able to resist Nebuchadnezzar's demand that they bow before his idol. But listen to their reasons for yourself:

> Shadrach, Meshach and Abednego replied to the king, "O Nebuchadnezzar, we do not need to defend ourselves before you in this matter. If we are thrown into the blazing furnace, the God we serve is able to save us from it, and he will rescue us from your hand, O king. But even if he does not, we want you to know, O king, that we will not serve your gods or worship the image of gold you have set up."

Note, first, that the three men stood together as one. "If *we* are thrown . . . the God *we* serve is able to save *us*. . . ." The Lone Ranger made for a great childhood hero, but you will search in vain for him here. God grants us tremendous power when we ally ourselves with others of like convictions.

Second, these men refused to be Sunday Christians, part-time pew sitters, or theoretical theologians. They exercised an active, dynamic faith, central to who they were: "the God we *serve*. . . ." Too many of us hop from church to church, searching for the best menus and cooks to "feed" us. We have forgotten what it is to serve. But if you want the strength to persevere in your faith, it is far better to wait on tables than to pat your belly.

Third, these men knew the power of God. They were not blind — they could see for themselves Nebuchadnezzar's fierce anger, his ferocious troops, and his bloodlust — yet their eyes took in nothing but the might and grandeur of Almighty God. "God . . . *is able to save us.* . . ." They did not look for an Israeli commando unit to shoot up the place with Uzis. They expected to see the omnipotent arm of God himself.

Fourth, they knew God loved them with an everlasting passion. It is one thing to notice a person's strength; it is another to hope that he will use that strength on your behalf. These men expected exactly that: "And *he will rescue us* from your hand, O king." They knew God well enough to expect a heavenly raiding party.

But that is not all they knew.

Last, and most importantly, these young men recognized that God was God, and they weren't. They fully expected Him to deliver them; but they left room for God's sovereign choice: "But *even if he does not,* we want you to know, O king, that we will not serve your gods or worship the image of gold you have set up."

But even if he does not. . . .

Shadrach, Meshach, and Abednego served God faithfully together. They basked in His love and remained confident of His power. They expected to see God respond in a powerful way to their very public faith. But they also knew that sometimes God asked His children to stiffen their backs, so they resolved to stand firm, come fire or freedom, death or deliverance. Long before the apostle Paul wrote the line, they expected that God would be glorified, "whether by life or by death" (see Phil. 1:20).

In their case, it was by life. But such is not always the outcome.

saws, whips, and chains

Hebrews 11 lists some of the Bible's most celebrated heroes. There you will read of Abel, Enoch, Noah, Abraham, Isaac, Jacob, Joseph, Moses, Rahab, and many more. The writer celebrates a ringing roll call of winners who "through faith conquered kingdoms, administered justice, and gained what was promised; who shut the mouths of lions, quenched the fury of the flames, and escaped the edge of the sword; whose weakness was turned to strength; and who became powerful in battle and routed foreign armies. Women received back their dead, raised to life again" (Heb. 11:33–35). The passage features more Special Deliveries and righteous reversals per square inch than any other literary real estate in the Bible.

But did you notice where I *stopped* quoting?

The remainder of the text is just as inspired, just as profitable for our growth, just as glorifying to God. But the room chills considerably on the other side of the divider: "Others were tortured and refused to be released, so that they might gain a better resurrection. Some faced jeers and flogging, while still others were chained and put in prison. They were stoned; they were sawed in two; they were put to death by the sword. They went about in sheepskins and goatskins, destitute, persecuted and mistreated — the world was not worthy of them. They wandered in deserts and mountains, and in caves and holes in the ground" (Heb. 11:35–38).

Quite a different picture, isn't it? How many Special Deliveries did you count in *that* passage?

By the way, don't take my question to be rhetorical; I don't assume the answer "none." Why not? Because despite appearances, the second passage boasts deliveries almost as divine as the first. They're just wearing disguises.

If you were to track down the individuals most likely mentioned in the second passage you would run into people such as Micaiah (find his story in 1 Kings 22), Jeremiah (Jer. 20), Zechariah (2 Chron. 24:17–27), Elijah (2 Kings 1), Isaiah (tradition says he was sawed in two), and even David (see chapter 8 of this book). All of these heroes of the faith saw God work in their lives in remarkable ways — and yet they themselves did not escape personal harm.

In the midst of the battle, these godly men suffered deep shrapnel wounds. Even so, if you asked them if the pain seemed worth it, I'm sure you'd hear a chorus of "You bet!" (in Hebrew, of course). That's what I mean by the agony of victory.

Four Verses from the End

I doubt whether this chapter brought you as much comfort as the previous ones were designed to do. I know I didn't have nearly as much fun writing it. Who likes pain and suffering? Those who do, we call masochists, and they aren't listed in any Bible concordance I know of.

All concordances *do* list the term "suffering," however. Multiple times. And while the Scriptures never lift up suffering as a biblical goal, suffering remains a biblical given. Consider Philippians 1:29: "For it has been granted to you on behalf of Christ not only to believe on him, but also to suffer for him." The same Word of God also points us to Colossians 1:28–29:

> We proclaim him [Christ], admonishing and teaching everyone with all wisdom, so that we may present everyone perfect in Christ. To this end I labor, struggling with all his energy, which so powerfully works in me.

This Colossians passage accurately describes the Agony of Victory, the long parade we've been watching. In verse 28 Paul described the *victory* he worked so hard to achieve: "That we may present everyone perfect in Christ." What a triumph! What an ending! What a grand finale to a glorious parade! But the Apostle knew he wouldn't reach the end of the march without some *agony* — in fact, the word translated "struggling" in verse 29 comes from the Greek term *agonizomai,* which eventually dropped into the English language as the word "agony."

Paul not only taught this stuff, he lived it. I won't take time now to review how deeply he lived it, but I do want to call attention to the words you'll find four verses from the end of his life.

The Apostle's final instruction to his contemporaries (and to us) is found in 2 Timothy. This would be the last book he wrote before the Romans cut short his days. Apparently he already felt the cold steel of the executioner's sword on his neck, for he wrote, "I am already being poured out like a drink offering, and the time has come for my departure" (2 Tim. 4:6).

He had fought the good fight; he had finished the race; he had kept the faith. Paul knew the end was near and that, this time, he could expect no Special Delivery. And yet, somehow, four verses from the end of his last letter, he has the chutzpah to write:

> The Lord will rescue me from every evil attack and will bring me safely to his heavenly kingdom. To him be glory for ever and ever. Amen (2 Tim. 4:18).

Now, it seems to me that execution by beheading should qualify as "an evil attack." I wouldn't put it in the "friendly greeting" category, would you? What's up here, anyway? We already saw that Paul knew he was about to die. It's even likely he could guess the means. So how could he say "the Lord will rescue me from every evil attack"?

I think he could say it because he believed with all his heart in the agony of victory.

He saw down the long corridor of time and was struck speechless at the final response God was preparing to his faith. His mind boggled at how all God's works throughout history were being woven by divine cunning into a stupendous, heart-stopping, faith-honoring event at the return of Christ. He insisted that although evil could touch him (when permitted), it could not ultimately hurt him. And he believed in *eucatastrophe,* a sudden turn of the story wherein darkness is turned to light and evil into good, where sorrow or failure is never denied but where a universal final defeat is.

That is, he believed in the God of the Bible.

So what sword that delivered Paul into his loving Father's arms could be called "evil"? The man who brandished the blade might give it such a name, but not the one who leapt, full of joy, from earth to heaven.

That is the agony of victory. There might be weeping in the night, but laughter greets the morning.

Your morning, too.

I don't deny your tears. I don't make light of your pain. But I *do* know that if you're marching in this parade right now, something phenomenal awaits you. For even though agony pushes its nose somewhere up toward the front, it's another three-syllable word that blows the final trumpet blast.

Vic • to • ry. And it's all yours.

questions for further study

1. Read Acts 14:21–22.
   A. Compare Acts 14:22 with Acts 14:19–20. How do these passages show that Paul understood "the agony of victory" long before his execution?
   B. The believers whom Paul and Barnabas addressed in Lystra and Iconium were fairly young in the faith. How does that make the statement in verse 22 so significant? Why would you say something like this to young believers?

2. Read 2 Timothy 2:8–10 and 3:10–12.
   A. What gave Paul the strength to pursue his ministry, according to 2 Timothy 2:8? Why does he tell us to consciously "remember" this information?
   B. What was Paul working so hard for (2 Tim. 2:10)? What kind of "glory" was he pursuing? How does this relate to "the agony of victory"?
   C. Why did Paul think it was wise to remind Timothy of what he suffered as an apostle (2 Tim. 3:10–11)?
   D. How does Paul apply the lessons of his own life to all Christians generally (2 Tim. 3:12)? Do you like this promise? Why or why not? What relationship does it have to "the agony of victory"?

why faith?

So God delights in honoring the faith of His people in strange and unexpected ways.

So what? Does this make any difference to the richness of our lives? We've learned that no one can predict where or when or how God will respond to genuine faith; so what advantage is there in believing that faith is stranger than fiction? If neither Christians nor pagans can be guaranteed a smooth road ahead, what advantage, then, is there in believing in the "strangeness" of faith?

To plagiarize the apostle Paul, "much in every way!"

Rather than list the enormous advantages, however, allow me to contrast the lives of two men profiled just weeks apart in *Sports Illustrated.* I think you'll begin to see what a massive difference it can make in *your* life.

two lives, two hopes

Old-timers with the New York Jets professional football team had never seen anything like it. As the year drew to a close, the organization's telephone system groaned under an onslaught of calls. One caller after another lit up the switchboard, asking the same thing: What could they do for Dennis?

The Dennis in question was Dennis Byrd, a 26-year-old defensive end for the Jets. Make that "former" defensive end. Even as the calls flooded in, Dennis was lying in Lenox Hill Hospital in New York City, partially paralyzed from a collision with teammate Scott Mersereau during a November 29, 1992, game against the Kansas City Chiefs.

"Maybe the fallen Byrd captured many hearts because of his matinee-idol looks," wrote *Sports Illustrated*.[1] "Or because people felt awful that another football player had been paralyzed. Or maybe it was something Byrd said when he was praying with some friends in his hospital room the night before he underwent a seven-hour operation to clear debris from his injured spinal column and stabilize his spine. 'God, I know you did this for a reason,' Byrd said. 'I'm your messenger.' Or maybe it was the message that Byrd's wife, Angela, sent by way of Jet kicker and family friend Cary Blanchard to the huge press contingent waiting for word, any word, on Dennis's condition. 'Tell them Dennis says he's glad God chose him for this, because he has the strength to handle it,' she said. 'And tell them I'm glad God chose me as Dennis's partner.' "

When Dennis wasn't on the field, it was a good bet you'd find him either with his family or with one of the many charities he supported. Byrd spearheaded a drive to establish a $15,000 scholarship fund to help needy children pay for tuition at a Bronx parochial school; he donated time and money to Forward Face, a charity for those with craniofacial disorders; he often assisted Survivors of the Shield, a New York charity for families of police officers killed or seriously hurt in action; he supported the Helen Keller Services for the Blind. In fact, the only time Byrd couldn't oblige a request to help a charity, he was taking his two-year-old daughter, Ashtin, to the Ice Capades.

Even while being transported to the hospital after his crippling injury, Byrd showed where his heart lay. Without tears he told his wife Angela that he knew he would never again play football; all he wanted to do, he said, was to be able to hold his girls. "We'll hold you," Angela replied.

Marvin Washington, Byrd's roommate on away games, confirmed Byrd's wholehearted commitment to his family:

> He's the real deal, man. The genuine article. Other guys talk about doing things for their family, but when you're around them, you can tell that's just words. Dennis lives it. He lives for his family.

Such commitment made a big impression on the whole team. For the remainder of the season, every Jet helmet featured a decal of Byrd's number 90 laid over an icthus, the ancient symbol of Christianity.

Byrd's faith guided him both before and after the accident — a faith full of the power of God. "Many times when his family, teammates, and coaches have visited Byrd in the hospital," said the article, "they have come away feeling as if *their* spirits had been lifted. 'We go in there wanting to help him,' says Blanchard, 'and he ends up helping us more.'"

I said that Byrd's strength and hope come from an unshakable trust in the God who loves to honor genuine faith, but don't take my word for it. I've never met the man. But writer Peter King has:

> Byrd says he has drawn strength from the biblical verse, written in black marker on white cardboard, that is hanging from the ceiling of his room at Lenox Hill. It's the first thing he sees whenever he wakes up — Romans 8:18: "For I reckon that the sufferings of this present time are not worthy to be compared with the glory which shall be revealed in us."

Friends, *that* is a man who firmly believes in the ability of God to turn sudden calamities into trophies of divine grace. He understands the agony of triumph. And his hospital room became a compelling argument for the strength and hope to be found in wholehearted devotion to the God who asks us to trust Him.

Let's now leave Dennis Byrd to meet another famous sport figure, profiled just a month later.

It sounds so silly now

The former North Carolina State basketball coach Jim Valvano is perhaps best known for leading his underdog Wolfpack to victory over the University of Houston in the 1983 NCAA Division I basketball finals. His verve, energy, and enthusiasm reached legendary proportions.

Less than a decade later he found himself fighting a different kind of opponent — the cancer which was eating its way through the marrow and bone of his spine. The article detailing Valvano's fight was titled simply "As Time Runs Out."[2] It began by recalling what made Valvano so successful as a college hoops coach:

> He didn't recruit kids to his college program; he swept them there. He walked into a prospect's home, and 15 minutes later he had rearranged the living-room furniture to demonstrate a defense, had Mom overplaying the easy chair, Dad on the lamp, Junior and his sister trapping the coffee table.
>
> Where the hell else was the kid going to go to school? In the 30 games Vee coached each season, the 100 speeches he eventually gave each year, the objective was the same: to make people leap, make them laugh, make them cry, make them dream, to move people. "Alive!" he would say. "That's what makes me feel alive!"

The author of the article, Gary Smith, then chronicled how Valvano lost his energy, his zest for living, and his hope. Smith asked:

> Didn't they understand? How could Vee allow himself to hope? If Vee liked a movie, he saw it five times. If Vee liked a song, he transcribed every word, memorized it, sang it 20 times a day and talked his kids into singing it with him a half dozen more times on the way to the beach. Vee couldn't throw half or three-quarters of his heart into anything; he had to throw it all. Didn't they know how dangerous it was for a man like him to throw all of his heart into a hope as slender as this? Vee was a dreamer. Vee had no life insurance. A man whose lows were as low as his highs were high couldn't hope too hard, couldn't lean too far, because the next downturn in his condition or the next darting away of his doctor's eyes could send him whirling down a shaft from which he might never escape.

Valvano's illness forced him to consider how he had spent his life. He didn't like what he found. One day he found himself poring over the season statistics of Iowa State guard Justus Thigpen before a national telecast, and he said:

> Justus Thigpen! Can you believe it? Who knows how much time I have left, and I've been sitting here poring over Justus Thigpen's stats in the Iowa State basketball brochure. I'm sitting here reading, and I quote, that "Justus Thigpen was twice selected Big Eight Player of the Week" and that "he scored 11 points at Kansas and 17 points in ISU's overtime win on ESPN versus Colorado." What the hell am I doing? The triviality of it just clobbers me. You get this sick and you say to yourself, "Sports means nothing," and that feels terrible . . . I devoted my whole life to it.

Valvano judged himself a terrible husband and father. He lamented that he had spent far too much time away from home — he wasn't even sure he knew his kids. For 23 years, he sacrificed his family at the altar of athletic success. He had a hard time believing what he'd done:

> I figured I'd have 20 years in the big time, who knows, maybe win three national titles, then pack it in at 53 or 54, walk into the house one day, put on a sweater and announce: "Here I am! Ozzie Nelson's here! I'm yours!" I always saw myself as becoming the all-time-great grandfather. Leave the kids with me? No problem. Crapped his pants? Fine, I'll change him. Vomited? Wonderful, I'll clean him up. I was going to make it up to them, all the time I'd been away. . . .
>
> God . . . it sounds so silly now. . . . But I didn't feel guilt about it then. My thinking always was, I would make a life so exciting that my wife and kids would be thrilled just to be a part of it. But I remember one Father's Day when I happened to be home,

and nobody had planned anything, nobody even mentioned it. How could they have planned anything? I'd probably never been home on Father's Day before. I might've been in Atlanta giving a Father's Day speech or in Chicago receiving a Father of the Year award, but you can bet I wasn't at home on Father's Day. Finally I asked them what we were going to do, and my daughter Jamie said, "Dad, we spent all our lives being part of your life. When are you going to be part of ours?" It hit me like a punch in the stomach.

Valvano grew more and more morose until one day he read a passage in a book by British sportswriter Brian Glanville. The passage said, "That is why athletics are important. They demonstrate the scope of human possibility, which is unlimited. The inconceivable is conceived, and then it is accomplished."

"That's it!" cried Vee. "That's why we strive! That's the value of sports! All those games, they mean nothing — and they mean everything!" His fist clenched. He hadn't poured himself into emptiness for 23 years, he hadn't devoured Justus Thigpen's stats for nothing, he hadn't. The people who compared his upset of Houston to his fight against cancer were right!

"It's what I've got to do to stay alive," he said. "I've got to find the unlimited scope of human possibility within myself. I've got to conceive the inconceivable — then accomplish it!"

Such was the slim hope to which Jim Valvano entrusted his very life. He wasn't a bad man for doing so, just one who grasped at whatever flimsy straws he could lay hold of. And I don't tell you his story so we can all shake our heads at what a wretch he was — all of us have done as badly, and perhaps worse. I rehearse Valvano's story simply to show what a vast difference it makes whether one trusts in the God who loves to honor genuine faith.

You can take your choice: dab on holy water four or five times a day while making the sign of the cross while desperately hoping that your will can whip the cancer cells ravaging your body; or wake up every day to the glorious sight of Romans 8:18, knowing that both your crippled body and your thriving soul are under the protective custody of the almighty King of the universe.

Which do you choose? It makes a world of difference.

But understand, too, that God seldom responds to our faith in the way we expect Him to. Some years ago I ran across the work of an anonymous Confederate soldier who understood this principle very well. His poem, written during the Civil War, reveals the heart of someone who has come to base his life on the conviction that faith is stranger than fiction.

I asked God for strength, that I might achieve;
I was made weak, that I might learn humbly to obey.
I asked for health, that I might do greater things;
I was given infirmity, that I might do better things.
I asked for riches, that I might be happy;
I was given poverty, that I might be wise.
I asked for power, that I might have the praise of men;
I was given weakness, that I might feel the need of God.
I asked for all things, that I might enjoy life;
I was given life, that I might enjoy all things.
I got nothing that I asked for — but everything I had hoped for.
Almost despite myself, my unspoken prayers were answered.
I am among all men, most richly blessed.

insight from the bible

Why does God declare such a love affair with faith? Why does He take such pleasure in honoring the faith of His children — yet do so in such strange and unexpected ways?

In short, why faith?

In this chapter I'd like to suggest that, through something as "weak" as faith, God can best display His limitless power and love. In a fallen world like this one, it is faith that best demonstrates His infinite worth. He wants our faith to magnify His greatness. Therefore, any time our faith magnifies us rather than Him, it short circuits God's intention, damages true faith, and ends up injuring us.

The Less the Evidence, the Better?

First things first. How does our Lord declare His fondness for faith?

One important text is found in John 20:29, where a resurrected Jesus told a "doubting" Thomas, "Because you have seen me, you have believed; blessed are those who have not seen and yet have believed."

This passage used to really puzzle me. It seemed to me that Jesus was telling His disciples that God promised some special benefit to those who would believe just for the sake of believing. The more the evidence, the less the blessing; the greater the leap of faith, the more God liked it.

I now think my early interpretation leaves a lot to be desired. Jesus never asked Thomas to believe just because it's cool to place your faith in stuff that lacks any evidence to back up its claims. Thomas had spent three full years with Jesus, watching Him perform miracle after miracle, listening to Him teach the very words of God, tasting the water that He had turned into wine. Thomas, along with the others, had heard Jesus predict many times that He would be crucified and rise from the dead on the third day. He had seen God work powerfully in Jesus' life, and he had been presented with more than enough evidence to trust the Lord's prophecies of His resurrection.

But despite all of that, he refused to believe.

When Jesus asks us to believe today, he doesn't request that we take a leap in the dark, any more than he made such a request of Thomas. He doesn't tell us that the less evidence for His claims, the more blessed we are to believe them. Rather, He calls us to faith on the same basis He called Thomas: consider His words; consider His miracles; consider His fulfilled prophecies. Today we have yet another source of evidence: how the power of God in Christ has changed the lives of countless millions through the ages.

But still we must make the same call that Thomas did.

Can we trust God for the future, based on what we saw in the past?

God loves our faith because it honors His faithfulness. When we believe His Word — however strange it may appear to us at the time — we bear witness that our Heavenly Father is worthy of all we have to give Him.

That's what the apostle Paul was getting at when he told the Corinthians, "For it seems to me that God has put us apostles on display at the end of the procession, like men condemned to die in the arena. We have been made a spectacle to the whole universe, to angels as well as to men" (1 Cor. 4:9). He means that our faith glorifies the majesty of God in the eyes of both men and angels.

And make no mistake, the angels — both good and evil — are watching! Speaking of the gospel, Peter tells us, "Even angels long to look into these things" (1 Pet. 1:12). In untold ages of existence, the angels have never seen the glory of God displayed in such a brilliant fashion as it is through the faith of God's people. The angels have never experienced faith personally; that's why it intrigues them.

And that's why the devil so incessantly attacks it.

Job, the Battleground

Go all the way back to the Book of Job, and you'll find Satan trying to undermine the faith of God's people. The *last* thing he wants is for our faith to magnify the greatness of God. He'd much rather prove that God is not so great after all, and that the faith of His people is but a sham. Consider just a few excerpts from that ancient book:

> Then the LORD said to Satan, "Have you considered my servant Job? There is no one on earth like him; he is blameless and upright, a man who fears God and shuns evil." "Does Job fear God for nothing?" Satan replied. "Have you not put a hedge around him and his household and everything he has? You have blessed the work of his hands, so that his flocks and herds are spread throughout the land. But stretch out your hand and strike every-

thing he has, and he will surely curse you to your face" (Job 1:8–11).

Do you see the devil's challenge? "You're not really so great, God. Job follows you only because of all the stuff you give him. Take that away, and watch his faith disappear. Then the whole universe will see how tarnished your 'glory' really is!"

The Lord allowed Satan to destroy everything Job possessed, including his family, but did not allow him to touch the man's body. When Job refused to turn his back on God, Satan came back for Round Two.

> Then the LORD said to Satan, "Have you considered my servant Job? There is no one on earth like him; he is blameless and upright, a man who fears God and shuns evil. And he still maintains his integrity, though you incited me against him to ruin him without any reason." "Skin for skin!" Satan replied. "A man will give all he has for his own life. But stretch out your hand and strike his flesh and bones, and he will surely curse you to your face." The LORD said to Satan, "Very well, then, he is in your hands; but you must spare his life" (Job 2:3–6).

If you've read the Book of Job, you know how the story turns out. While Job expresses many angry questions, he refuses to abandon his faith in God. In the end, the Lord shows Job His glory — the glory Satan tried to defame — Job shuts his mouth, and God rewards faithful Job with double the possessions he owned before the calamity.

And somewhere far beyond all earthly dimensions, the watching angels learned a little bit about how something as weak as faith could spotlight the glory of God. It was like nothing they'd ever seen.

weak faith, strong god

Because faith is nothing but a channel through which the power of God can flow, it works best in weak vessels. So Paul could say, "But we have this treasure in jars of clay to show that this all-surpassing power is from God and not from us" (2 Cor. 4:7).

If Paul were strong, people (and angels) might say, "His God is not so great; he does most of that stuff on his own." But when people (and angels) see the power of God demonstrated through a "jar of clay" armed with nothing but faith, they can't say any such thing. In that case they know the only explanation for what they see is the marvelous power of Almighty God.

And He gets the glory.

Turning Evil Inside Out

Through the faith of His people, the Lord loves to take the devil's most abominable schemes and transform them into spectacles of God's glory. Time after time in biblical history we see this pattern:

- Pharaoh's decree to kill all Jewish newborn boys directly resulted in the nurture, education, and training of Moses — all at the expense of the Egyptian royal household (Exod. 1).

- When the Philistines finally captured Samson, they gouged out his eyes, shackled him, threw him into prison, and rejoiced that "our god has delivered Samson, our enemy, into our hands." But later when Samson was brought out to be mocked, the Lord gave him superhuman strength one last time so that "he killed many more when he died than while he lived" (Judg. 16).

- A plot by jealous court officials managed to get Daniel tossed into a den of lions. But God kept him from harm, while the men who plotted his death were themselves later seized and thrown into the lions' den, "and before they reached the floor of the den, the lions overpowered them and crushed all their bones" (Dan. 6).

- Saul of Tarsus promoted a bloody persecution of Christians, beginning with the stoning of Stephen and culminating in the dispersion of the young church, many of whose members fled to Antioch. Yet a few years later God turned this violent persecutor into a mighty apostle and sent him to Antioch to build up the church he once destroyed (Acts 7, 11:26).

Wherever we look in Scripture, we see how God delights in using the "strange" faith of His people to wreck Satan's schemes and spotlight His glory. But why does God seem to follow this pattern so often? What is it about turning the devil's most fiendish schemes inside out that gives God so much delight?

fitting the puzzle together

I think we can guess the answer by considering several Scriptures together. First, from Isaiah:

> I am the LORD; that is my name! I will not give my glory to another or my praise to idols (Isa. 42:8).

> For my own sake, for my own sake, I do this. How can I let myself be defamed? I will not yield my glory to another (Isa. 48:11).

God will not permit anyone to defame His name or rob Him of the praise due that name. And he absolutely will not share His glory with anyone else — as if anyone else were His equal. God has no peers. He, alone, is God. He is utterly unique. That is why He will share His glory with no one.

With that piece of the puzzle in place, let's consider two more passages that may help us to understand a bit more.

> The arrogance of man will be brought low and the pride of man humbled; the LORD alone will be exalted on that day (Isa. 2:17).

> God opposes the proud but gives grace to the humble (1 Pet. 5:5).

The question here is, "Why does God oppose the proud? What is so bad about pride? And what is so good about humility?"

I think the answer is that proud people try to pass themselves off as God's rivals. Consciously or not, they see themselves as God's peers. In their arrogance they lust for the praise that belongs to God alone. And therefore God makes it His special aim to bring them low, to humble them — to show the world He has no equals. The humble already know this. They know they are but creatures and they are happy to be so. Through faith, they love to honor God as the only majestic One — and that is why God loves to honor *them*.

So now we are close to discovering why God loves to turn Satan's schemes inside out. The final Scripture I want to consider is 1 Corinthians 1:25:

> For the foolishness of God is wiser than man's wisdom, and the weakness of God is stronger than man's strength.

Now, I admit that this text speaks of *man's* wisdom and *man's* strength, not Satan's. But surely it is as true in the demonic realm as it is in the human. Who would say that Satan is stronger or wiser than God? God has no equals, no rivals, no peers. Not in the human sphere and not in the demonic.

So with this third piece of the puzzle in place, we can at last try to see why God takes such great delight in honoring His people's faith by turning inside out the devil's wicked schemes.

glory! glory! hallelujah!

God has declared throughout Scripture that His goal is to showcase His majesty and glory. He has no rivals; He stands alone, absolutely unique. In fact, He is committed with all His infinite power to exalting His own name and humbling all pretenders. "I will not yield my glory to another" (Isa. 48:11). "The LORD alone will be exalted in that day" (Isa. 2:11, 2:17). The devil, on the other hand, has long wished to usurp God's place (Matt. 4:8–11; 2 Thess. 2:4; Rev. 13:4). This God will never permit.

So, what better way to humble the proud — in this case, the devil — than to turn his own, most potent schemes against him? What better way for God to show His strength than to pit his "weakness" (the faith of His people) against Satan's "strength" . . . and win? How better to showcase His glory than to provide example after example that "the foolishness of God is wiser than Satan's wisdom, and the weakness of God is stronger than Satan's strength"?

It is very much like what God did to Pharaoh at the time of the Exodus. God, through Moses, demanded that Pharaoh release the Israelites. But Pharaoh refused. "Who is the LORD, that I should obey him and let Israel go?" he asked. "I do not know the LORD and I will not let Israel go" (Exod. 5:2). Ten times Moses implored him to release the people, and ten times he refused. To an uninformed observer, it looked as if Pharaoh was successfully thwarting God's plans. The strength of Pharaoh and the might of the Lord were pitted against each other, and it appeared as if Pharaoh were winning.

But not in the topsy-turvy world where faith is stranger than fiction. It turned out that even Pharaoh was merely a tool in God's hand. This is what the Lord himself had to say about the stubborn Egyptian king:

> I have raised you up for this very purpose, that
> I might show you my power and that my name might
> be proclaimed in all the earth (Exod. 9:16).

In other words, even Pharaoh's stubbornness and pride would, in the end, serve God's purposes. God knew that immediately after Pharaoh liberated the Israelites, the king would change his mind and send his army to annihilate God's people. But even *this* would play into God's hands:

> But I will gain glory for myself through Pharaoh and all his army, and the Egyptians will know that I am the Lord (Exod. 14:4).

And that is exactly what happened. The proud forces of humankind's mightiest ruler perished beneath the surging waves of an angry sea. Chariots and horses and spears and arrows are no match for a watery torrent obedient to every whisper of God's voice. If only Pharaoh had believed that faith is stranger than fiction! But he didn't.

Oh, make sure that you don't follow his foolish example!

The Bottom Line

Why faith? Why does God so love to honor the faith of His people, especially in using Satan's worst schemes against him?

It comes down to this: through faith, we have the opportunity to show men and angels the greatness of our God. Our Lord invites us to dip into His glory, through faith, and so bring light to a dark world.

Some might think that sounds like a strange plan, but for those of us who have tasted even a little of that glory, I think it sounds downright delicious.

Questions for Further Study

1. Read Isaiah 42:8 and 48:9–11.
   A. Compare Isaiah 42:8 with John 17:4–5. What claim was Jesus making in His prayer?
   B. Remembering that Isaiah 42 is a prophecy of the coming Messiah, compare verse 8 with verses 3 and 7. How do these verses, taken together, show that God's concern for His glory is not a vain thing but a tremendously encouraging one?
   C. How does Isaiah 48:9–11 teach us that the foundation of our salvation is found in God's concern for His glory?

2. Read Isaiah 2:12–17 and 1 Peter 5:5–6.
   A. What does Isaiah 2:12–17 teach us about God's attitude toward pride? How will He eventually deal with it?
   B. What does Peter mean that God "opposes" the proud? What does he mean that God "gives grace" to the humble? What promise does he report in verse 6? In what way(s) can this be an enormously practical verse?

3. Read 1 Corinthians 1:25–31.
   A. Why did God choose the "foolish things" of the world (verse 27)? Why did He choose the "weak things," the "lowly things," the "despised things," and the "things that are not"?

B. How do verses 25 through 28 "set up" Paul's comment of verse 29? In what way does God make sure that no one is able "to boast before him"?

C. In what way is verse 31 a good summary of the bedrock reason why God delights in faith and in acting for those who place their trust in Him?

12

Coming Attractions

Anticipation — it's a big part of what makes coming attractions so inviting. When we catch some glimpse of the great things coming our way, we naturally get excited.

Remember your first few Christmases? Or your first day at school? The time your family scheduled a trip to Disneyland, or when you were getting ready for your first real date?

Anticipation!

You could hardly wait for the big day to arrive. You dreamed about it, talked about it, fantasized about it. In fact, you couldn't stop yourself. It constantly filled your mind and kept the goose bumps dimpling your flesh.

That's the way I'd like you to feel about the "coming attractions" God is even now sending your way. So far we've considered a lot of uplifting stories about how faith is stranger than fiction in the lives of God's children throughout the world. Now it's time to focus on *you*, on the strange-but-wonderful ways God intends to honor *your* faith.

There's only one problem: I have no idea what God might be up to. Not in your life, and not even in mine. How can I describe events that have yet to happen?

Quite simply, I can't. But I *can* look back to the expectations of men and women who knew they were about to step through the doorway of death, the most personal "coming attraction" of all. And I can ask, "How did their faith — or lack of it — shape their reaction to this most awesome of coming events? And what can their words tell us about living by faith *right now*, before we see death making a beeline for *us*?"

In other words, I'd like to glimpse our future by viewing the past. And I want to encourage all of us to keep living by faith, whatever our circumstances, by remembering the last words of dozens of men and women who have gone ahead of us.

Before we get to the "good stuff," however, let's make sure we understand what's really at stake.

faithless words

When the day comes for you to check out of this world and into the next, will you be ready? Will your faith sustain you in that hour, when shadows lengthen and earthly voices grow dim?

History records many sad instances of those who failed to prepare. Many of these dying men and women spent much of their lives arrogantly ridiculing people of faith.

But all things come to an end.

Flavius Claudius Julianus, a Roman emperor known as "Julian the apostate" for his futile attempts to restore pagan religion throughout his empire, died while on a military campaign in Persia. After years spent opposing and persecuting Christians, his last recorded words were directed to Jesus himself: "You have conquered, O Galilean!"

He didn't say it happily.

The sultan of Spain, Caliph Abd-er-Rahman III, died in A.D. 961. In his long rule he had acquired vast riches and great fame. But despite all this, he died an unhappy man. "Fifty years have passed since first I was caliph," he said on his deathbed. "Riches, honors, pleasures — I have enjoyed them all. In this long time of seeming happiness I have numbered the days on which I have been happy: *14!*"

What a sad, sad commentary — and yet, more sad still, not an uncommon one. The king of France, Phillip III, fared little better than did the sultan. As he lay dying he cried out, "What an account I shall have to give to God! How I should like to live otherwise than I have lived." But it was too late.

Of course, it's not only the wealthy and powerful who fritter away their lives in vain pursuits. A criminal named Captain John Lee was executed for his offenses, and as death approached, he sought in vain for comfort: "I leave to the world this mournful memento, that however much a man may be favored by personal qualifications or distinguished mental endowments, genius will be useless, and abilities avail little, unless accompanied by religion and attended by virtue. Oh, that I had possession of the meanest place in heaven, and could but creep into one corner of it."

But heaven is not a place to "creep into." Either one enters it joyfully and triumphantly, through faith, or not at all. I fear that Mr. Lee never found his corner.

Claudius Salmasius earned a formidable reputation as a scholar of French classics. But despite the accolades he received in his distinguished career, he died with a stricken conscience. "I have lost a world of time!" he moaned. "Had I one year more, it should be spent in perusing David's psalms and Paul's epistles. Mind the world less, and God more."

Salmasius wasn't the only literary figure to lament a wasted life. Even today Edward Gibbon's *Decline and Fall of the Roman Empire* remains a gem of historiography, though it was written more than two centuries ago. Yet its author never embraced the gospel of Christ, and he died a frightened and gloomy man. He told those gathered around his deathbed, "This day may be my last. I will agree that the immortality of the soul is at times a very comfortable doctrine. All this is now lost, finally, irrevocably lost. All is dark and doubtful."

And then he died.

Thomas Paine earned a worldwide reputation as an author and skeptic through the publication of several books and tracts in the late 17th century. But when he died in 1809, he perished unhappy and fearful. As he saw the curtain being drawn on his earthly years, he lamented, "I would give worlds, if I had them, that *Age of Reason* had not been published. O Lord, help me! Christ, help me! O God, what have I done to suffer so much? But there is no God! But if there should be, what will become of me hereafter? Stay with me, for God's sake! Send even a child to stay with me, for it is hell to be alone. If ever the devil had an agent, I have been that one."

Not exactly the way I want to go. A life of faith may sometimes seem hard — but to die without faith brings infinitely worse consequences.

An English poet and satirist named Charles Churchill made that terrible discovery. He died in 1764 after devoting his life to wild living and clever scorn of the Christian lifestyle. But a lifetime of mocking all things godly takes its toll. With his last breath he confessed, "What a fool I have been."

The French noblewoman Vicomtesse D'Houdetot left this world in a similar way by saying simply, "I regret my life."

Regret. Fear. Foolishness. The legacy of a lifetime spent pursuing everything but God. One of the saddest of all these sobering accounts is that of William Pope, a contemporary of Thomas Paine. Pope earned fame as part of a group of men who loved to ridicule religion. Sometimes, as a game, they would kick a Bible around the floor or tear it up. But as Pope died, the laughter fled from his throat. Only terror remained: "I have no contrition. I cannot repent. God will damn me. I know the day of grace is past. . . . You see one who is damned forever. . . . Oh, eternity! Eternity! . . . Nothing for me but hell. Come, eternal torments. . . . I hate everything God has made, only I have no hatred for the devil — I wish to be with him. I long to be in hell. Do you not see? Do you not see him? He is coming for me."

I wonder — who is coming for *you?*

Throughout these pages we have been saying that faith is stranger than fiction. What we have not said is that faithlessness is deadlier than fiction.

These people all died with fear in their eyes and raking anguish in their hearts. Yet it didn't have to be that way. They, too, could have lived in the confidence that faith is stranger than fiction, that God honors the simple trust of His children, and that death can be faced not only with courage, but with joy.

Joy! That's what erupts when stranger-than-fiction faith transforms death into a heavenly coming attraction.

The voice of joy

Before there was Billy Graham, there was D.L. Moody. God used this former shoe salesman to awaken spiritually slumbering individuals on two continents with the good news of the gospel. He died in 1899 at the age of 62, but in death as in life, he proclaimed the same hopeful message. With his last few ragged breaths, he declared, "I see earth receding; heaven is opening. God is calling me."

It's good to know who is calling you, but it's also good to know where you're going. John Bunyan, the celebrated author of the Christian allegory *Pilgrim's Progress*, died in 1628 after visiting London to help a distraught father reconcile with his estranged son. On his return home, a wild storm soaked Bunyan to the skin and he came down with a mysterious illness. Ten days later he died. But he did not leave this world before he had once more strengthened the faith of his loved ones. On his deathbed he said to them, "Weep not for me, but for yourselves. I go to the Father of our Lord Jesus Christ; who will, no doubt, through the mediation of His blessed Son, receive me, though a sinner: when I hope we shall ere long meet to sing the new song, and remain everlastingly happy, world without end. Amen!"

While the death of a believer is a going, it's also a coming. Charles Wesley, the hymn-writing brother of evangelist John Wesley, knew this. Just before he died at age 77, he said, "Come, my dearest Jesus, the nearer the more precious, the more welcome. I cannot contain it! What manner of love is this to a poor worm? I cannot express the thousandth part of what praise is due to Thee. It is but little I can give Thee, but Lord, help me to give Thee my all. I will die praising Thee, and rejoice that others can praise Thee better. I shall be satisfied with Thy likeness! Satisfied! Satisfied! O my dearest Jesus, I come."

John Wesley founded the Methodist Church and, through his ceaseless evangelistic labors, is probably more responsible for saving England from a bloody revolution than any other man. He died with praise and glory on his lips. As he saw death approaching, he summoned up his strength one last time and cried out, "The best of all is, God is with us. The best of all is, God is with us." He paused, then said, "Farewell!" With that, he joined his Maker in heaven.

Other itinerant preachers also knew how to die well. William Gadsby traveled some 60,000 miles on horseback to deliver about 12,000 sermons. He won such a devoted following that 30,000 people attended his funeral in 1844. Bystanders recorded his last, triumphant message: "I shall soon be with Him. Victory, victory, victory!" Then he raised his hand and spoke one final word: "*Forever!*"

Catherine Booth, wife of the founder of the Salvation Army, comforted her loved ones with the following last words: "The waters are rising, but so am I. I am not going under but over. Do not be concerned about dying; go on living well, the dying will be right."

Samuel Rutherford, author of a famous series of *Letters* written from prison to former parishioners, modeled Christlike compassion and conviction throughout his 61 years of life. When the pro-Roman Catholic Charles II returned to the English throne in 1660, Rutherford and other Presbyterians fell into great danger. Parliament summoned the Scottish minister to appear before it to answer to the charge of high treason, but he died before he could make the trip. He sent this message in his place: "Tell the Parliament that I have received a summons to a higher bar. I must needs answer that first, and when the day you name shall come, I shall be where few of you shall enter. Oh, dear brethren, preach for Christ, feed the flock of God! Oh, beware of men-pleasing! Glory! Glory!"

The "missionary apostle to Burma," Adoniram Judson, continues to hold an honored place in the history of modern missions. He died at sea in 1850 while attempting to sail to the Isle of Bourbon, despite poor health. Before he left this earth, he declared to his shipmates, "I go with the gladness of a boy bounding away from school, I feel so strong in Christ."

A former governor of Massachusetts, John Brooks, said on his deathbed in 1825, "I see nothing terrible in death. I'm looking to the future; I have no fears. I know in whom I believed. I look back upon my past life with humility. I am sensible of many imperfections that cleave to me. I now rest my soul on the mercy of my Creator, through the only mediator, His Son, our Lord. Oh, what a ground of hope there is in that saying of Paul that God is in Christ reconciling the guilty world to himself, not imputing their trespasses unto them!"

Although "Rock of Ages" first appeared back in 1776, many believers still count the hymn among their all-time favorites. The hymn's writer, Augustus Montague Toplady, died of an illness just two years after publishing his famous composition. Moments before he passed away he awoke from sleep and said, "Oh, what delights! Who can fathom the joy of the third heaven? The sky is clear, there is no cloud; come, Lord Jesus, come quickly!" He grew quiet, then spoke his final words: "No mortal man can live after the glories which God has manifested to my soul."

Donald Cargill died in the Scottish religious persecutions of the 17th century. Renowned as a powerful preacher, he was condemned as a traitor and hurried off to the gallows. Before he died, he sang a part of Psalm 118. Then he declared for everyone to hear, "Now I am near to getting to my crown, which shall be sure; for I bless the Lord, and desire all of you to bless Him that He hath brought me here, and makes me triumph over devils, and men, and sin! They shall wound me no more. I forgive all men the wrongs they have done to me, and pray the Lord may forgive all the wrongs that any of the elect have done against Him. I pray that sufferers may be kept from sin, and helped to know their duty. . . . Farewell, reading and preaching, praying and believing, wanderings, reproaches, and sufferings. Welcome joy unspeakable and full of glory!"

As the writer to the Hebrews said, "All these people were still living by faith when they died" (Heb. 11:13). Like the great saints of the Old Testament, these men and women "through faith conquered kingdoms, administered justice, and gained what was promised." Their "weakness was turned to strength," while some "were tortured and refused to be released, so that they might gain a better resurrection" (Heb. 11:33–35). Like their predecessors in faith, "the world was not worthy of them" (Heb. 11:38).

And like their spiritual forebears, "these were all commended for their faith" (Heb. 11:39). By whom?

By God himself!

That same God invites you and me to follow in their train. God loves to honor us, His children, for our childlike faith in Him. He loves to show us how simple faith can trigger stranger-than-fiction events that shock the world. And He especially loves to demonstrate what He meant when He inspired the touching words, "Precious in the sight of the LORD is the death of his saints" (Ps. 116:15).

Through faith, we can even now begin to prepare ourselves for the day when we must walk through death's doorway and into the greatest coming attraction of all.

We can follow the example of Arthur Triggs, who came to faith as a 19 year old after meditating on the word "eternity." When the time came, 53 years later, for his Lord to call him home, he announced, "If any friends ask about me, tell them it is sweet to die in Jesus. Oh, I am longing to be with Him. He is my Redeemer." A few moments later he called out, "Come, Lord Jesus!" And then he was gone.

We can join the chorus brightened by Samuel Medley, a hymnwriter born in Hertfordshire, England, in 1738. Medley died at age 61 after dedicating his life to exalting the grace of God and promoting personal holiness. As he crossed from one world to another he said in a calm, sure voice, "Dying is sweet work! Sweet work! My heavenly Father, I am looking up to my dear Jesus, my God, my portion, my all in all. Glory, glory, home, home!"

And we can echo the hope spoken by a scholarly Methodist preacher named Dinsdale T. Young, who said just two words as God called him home: "I triumph!"

But in order to triumph *then*, we must live by faith *now*. Only in that way can we avoid saying something like those immortal words screeched by the dying Mexican bandit Pancho Villa: "Don't let it end like this. Tell them I said something!"

That's not strange so much as it is ridiculous. Guard against saying anything so silly on your deathbed by placing your full trust in the God who loves to honor your faith. And keep at it until the final coming attraction becomes a present reality.

That won't be strange, either. That'll be just plain fabulous!

Insight from the Bible

The best thing about some movies is the trailer — the slick, entertaining preview of an upcoming film designed to whet the appetites of paying audiences. Trailers often feature the funniest, most explosive, or outrageous clips from a yet-to-be-released movie.

Some time ago I saw a trailer for a film to be released around Christmas. In it the star of the picture, a zany stand-up comedian, delivered line after line of gut-busting silliness. No props. No costumes. Not even any clips from the movie. Just the performer hamming it up in the middle of a wheat field.

The audience howled. I've never seen a stronger reaction to any coming attraction. We clapped, we roared, we shook the seats. The lady behind me screeched through the whole trailer.

A few weeks later I saw a different trailer for the same movie, this one featuring actual film clips. No one laughed. I heard not a chortle, not even a giggle.

Can you say, "Bomb"?

I'm glad I didn't see that film, but other trailers have completely deceived me. I plunked down my money hoping to see some smash-up entertainment, and left with only my hopes smashed. Just imagine how great it would be to live in a world where even excellent trailers didn't begin to match up to the real thing. Envision a company that unfailingly produced blockbuster movies as well as terrific teasers. Then suppose you could see these awesome previews right now, at no charge.

But it could never be. Could it?

Well, I have my doubts about a movie company, but I'm certain the "blockbuster" and "preview" parts are absolutely true. In fact, I'm familiar with several previews of coming attractions that, while awesome in themselves, can only hint at the power of the real thing. And you don't even have to visit a theater to enjoy them.

All you have to do is open your Bible.

Since God does not change (Mal. 3:6) and "is the same yesterday and today and forever" (Heb. 13:8), we might have expected to discover that, in the future, God's response to the faith of His people will continue to be stranger than fiction.

Maybe even more strange!

The coveted oholiabs?

If Hollywood has its Oscars, I think there's a good chance heaven has its Oholiabs.

The Academy of Motion Picture Arts and Sciences began awarding its gold-plated statuette in 1927, but the trophy did not receive the name "Oscar" until 1931. That year when someone showed a trophy to Mrs. Margaret Herrick, librarian of the Academy, she responded, "He reminds me of my Uncle Oscar."

The name stuck. A local newspaper columnist heard the comment and soon informed his readers that "Employees of the Academy have affectionately dubbed their famous statuette 'Oscar.' "[1]

In other words, the term is essentially meaningless. (There's a parable in there somewhere.)

On the other hand, consider the Oholiab. What a great name that would be for an award given to honor all the faithful servants of God who labor for the kingdom! We first read about Oholiab in Exodus 31:1–6. In that passage the Lord tells Moses to appoint a man named Bezalel "to make artistic designs for work in gold, silver and bronze, to cut and set stones, to work in wood, and to engage in all kinds of craftsmanship." God tells Moses that He filled Bezalel with His Spirit and that this artist had been given skill, ability, and knowledge in all kinds of crafts . . . and that God had appointed a certain man named Oholiab to help him out.

Oholiab gets mentioned just five times in the Bible, each time in connection with his sacred work. Exodus 38:23 gives the most detailed profile of the man: "Oholiab son of Ahisamach, of the tribe of Dan — a craftsman and designer, and an embroiderer in blue, purple and scarlet yarn and fine linen."

I think it would be just like God to name heaven's award after this excellent man. The Oholiab would represent all those throughout human history who have faithfully labored for their heavenly Master, in whatever capacity or calling He chose for them. They're not superstars. They're not famous. They don't have fan clubs and they're not consumed with building an empire or getting rich. What *does* consume them is faithful obedience to the God of the universe.

And that's why, regardless of the existence of a heavenly reward named the Oholiab, God has committed himself to rewarding His faithful people beyond their wildest dreams.

One thing is for sure: unlike Hollywood's extravaganza, tickets will be plentiful for heaven's version of the Academy Awards. The only requirement will be residence inside the pearly gates (Rev. 22:14–17). Whosoever will may come; whosoever won't may not.

Another difference may also be among the most intriguing. While Oscar kicks up his heels every year, the Oholiab would have but one moment in the sun.

But what a blazing, glorious moment it would be!

Think of it: millions of Oholiabs even now stored away in vast, celestial treasure houses, waiting for the moment when the Lord himself, as master of ceremonies, calls name upon name of His faithful children to receive their due. The apostle Paul described the scene like this:

> For we must all appear at the judgment seat of Christ, that each one may receive what is due him for the things done while in the body, whether good or bad (2 Cor. 5:10).

Every Oholiab would be for lifetime achievement, but not every resident of heaven will get one. Some will come to the ceremonies and have a good time, but leave empty-handed. Oh, they'll be glad they were able to attend, but they'll never get to set one of the prized trophies on the mantle of their new mansion. It'll be too late. Whether any of us will receive an Oholiab depends entirely on how we choose to live out our faith while still on earth.

Do some of us feel tempted to give up because God doesn't respond to our faith in the way we desire? Are we ready to pull ourselves out of contention for the Oholiab because our suffering and pain make no sense to us?

Hold on! The more I see God at work, the more I see that it is *only* at this awards ceremony that we will finally learn why God allowed some catastrophes to wallop us. It will only be as we stand before the King of the universe, Oholiab in His hand, that we will start to understand the real stakes involved in our day-to-day lives. And it will only be as we leave the stage, Oholiab in *our* hands — with throngs of angels and the redeemed applauding our faithful efforts — that we will see how strange faith really can be.

Some of us might be tempted to ask the emcee on that day, "Lord, why didn't you give me at least *some* hint about what You were doing in my life during those especially hard years?" But even if we were still interested in posing such a question, I think He would answer much as He did while Jesus walked among us: "Child, I had much to tell you, but you could not bear it then" (see John 16:12).

It may be that only at these ceremonies will the great saints of Hebrews 11 finally see the exclamation point placed at the end of their biblical commendation:

> These were all commended for their faith, yet none of them received what had been promised. God had planned something better for us so that only together with us would they be made perfect (Heb. 11:39–40).

I think Jesus implied something like this when He taught that faithful service in small things will result one day in ruling many "cities" (Luke 19:11–19; see also 2 Tim. 2:12; Rev. 5:10, 20:6, 22:5)). Maybe, just maybe, some of the severe training exercises arranged for us down here are not meant to teach us anything at all about life on this world; perhaps the hard lessons will become useful only in our new, eternal occupations. We may not be running cities now, but a good mayor knows the importance of a first-rate sewage disposal system. Perhaps God thinks it best that we learn our jobs from the ground up.

God awards His trophies not to fast starters, but to faithful finishers. Our Lord lets us see that faith is stranger than fiction just enough to encourage us to continue running the race. Sometimes we don't finish the last lap until heaven. Genuine faith implies temporary pain, but promises eventual glory.

Are you looking forward to that glory? Are you living today in a way that will win you heaven's prize tomorrow?

Do you want an Oholiab?

Remember, the only people who get them are those who,

in faith, entrust their lives to the Lord of the cosmos. Happy are they who walk hand in hand with God, even when the way is hard and faith seems more agonizing than strange.

I'm sure the apostle Peter was looking forward to receiving his award. He also wanted his friends to enjoy the same honor. At the end of his second letter (and his life), he wrote:

> But the day of the Lord will come like a thief. The heavens will disappear with a roar; the elements will be destroyed by fire, and the earth and everything in it will be laid bare. Since everything will be destroyed in this way, what kind of people ought you to be? You ought to live holy and godly lives as you look forward to the day of God and speed its coming (2 Pet. 3:10–12).

Holy and godly lives make for a prized Oholiab on the mantle of your very own heavenly mansion. They're well worth anything we're called to suffer, even if God doesn't seem to be responding to your faith as you'd like Him to.

So go after your Oholiab with everything that's in you! Don't let the disappointments (or the successes) of life "down here" steal the spotlight awaiting you "up there." Don't let the allure of earthly riches or fame or "success" rob you of the honor God wants to bestow upon you in heaven.

In other words, don't be like Napoleon.

Our textbooks may honor Napoleon, but I doubt he'll ever get an Oholiab. He spent most of his life trying to win glory for himself, not for the God who honors genuine faith. The "Little General" chose his own route.

But at least by the end of his life he understood that godly living brings the only real rewards, that the Lord loves to honor the faith of His children in strange and unexpected ways . . . and that Jesus Christ rules. Just before his death, Napoleon made this remarkable confession:

> I die before my time and my body shall be given back to the earth and devoured by worms. What an abysmal gulf between my deep miseries and the eternal

Kingdom of Christ! I marvel that whereas the ambitious dreams of myself and Alexander and of Caesar should have vanished into thin air, a Judean peasant, Jesus, should be able to stretch His hands across the centuries, and control the destinies of men and nations.[2]

I marvel, too. Don't you? That Jesus really gets around. But what Napoleon couldn't explicitly say was that the Master controls *your* destiny, too.

The Oholiab, however, is a slightly different matter. You can choose to give him a place on your heavenly mantle, or you can practice dusting the bare spot where he could have been.

Be wise and forget the Lemon Pledge!

Questions for further study

1. Read 2 Corinthians 5:1–10.
   A. How does Paul characterize life "down here" (verses 2–4)?
   B. According to verse 5, what is one purpose for which God made us? How is the fulfillment of this purpose guaranteed?
   C. Why should we make it our goal to please God by the way we live (verses 9–10)? How many people will receive what is "due" them at the judgment seat of Christ? What does the phrase imply, "whether good or bad"? How does this judgment make you feel? Why?

2. Read Luke 19:11–27.
   A. Retell this story in your own words. What characters are involved? What do they do? How does it end?
   B. In what way is this story a graphic illustration of 2 Corinthians 5:10? How does it illustrate Paul's phrase, "whether good or bad"? How does this story make you feel? Why?
   C. What is the overriding principle of this passage? What exhortation does it give? Should all the details of this parable be taken literally? Why or why not?

3. Read 2 Peter 3:10–15 and 18.

    A. What "coming attraction" does this passage highlight? What is to happen?

    B. How is this "coming attraction" supposed to affect the way we live today as believers in Jesus Christ (verses 11–14)?

    C. Why does the Lord wait to bring on this event, according to verse 15? What does this imply about what we ought to be doing?

    D. Has this book helped you to follow Peter's direction in verse 18? If so, how? In what way will your increased knowledge or graciousness change the way you live or interact with those around you?

Epilogue

The Strangest
Thing of All

for as long as God has sought out a people for His name, strange things have been going on. Have you ever stopped to think about that? Often we get so used to the rhythms of our faith that we forget just how surprising the whole thing really is. Go all the way back to Moses, and how does God first get the man's attention? Through something surpassingly *strange*.

> Now Moses was tending the flock of Jethro his father-in-law, the priest of Midian, and he led the flock to the far side of the desert and came to Horeb, the mountain of God. There the angel of the LORD appeared to him in flames of fire from within a bush. Moses saw that though the bush was on fire it did not burn up. So Moses thought, "I will go over and see this *strange sight* — why the bush does not burn up" (Exod. 3:1–3, italics added).

In God's plan, it was something strange that led to the Exodus, that crowning event of the Old Testament, itself filled with strange happenings (rivers turning to blood, sticks turning into snakes, seas piling up in a heap, etc.). The prophet Isaiah noticed this pattern of strangeness, too, and couldn't help but comment on it:

The LORD will rise up as he did at Mount Perazim, he will rouse himself as in the Valley of Gibeon — to do his work, his *strange work* (Isa. 28:21, italics added).

Centuries later, by the time the Holy Spirit is poured out on the church at Pentecost, the Apostles seem to think that *nothing* God does ought to surprise anyone. And that includes the healing of a man over 40 years of age who had been crippled since birth:

Peter . . . said to them, "Men of Israel, why does this surprise you? Why do you stare at us as if by our power or godliness we had made this man walk? The God of Abraham, Isaac and Jacob, the God of our fathers, has glorified his servant Jesus" (Acts 3:12–13).

God continues to do strange things today in response to the faith of His dearly loved people. If it takes a burning bush, He lights it up without burning it up. If it takes judgment, He sends in the heavenly troops. If it takes a miraculous healing, he makes lame men leap and dance and sing.

Strange? From our perspective, sure. But from God's viewpoint, all these "strange" events make perfect sense. He wants to cultivate a people who will trust Him no matter what, and strangeness (applied in the proper amounts) seems to build our faith like nothing else.

Do you want to know what's *really* strange, though? It's not the surprising answers God sometimes gives to our prayers. It's not the unexpected ways He chooses to build our faith. It's not even the weird events He arranges to honor our faith and bring himself glory.

It's the fact that He wants us at all. And not only wants us, but loves us enough to send His beautiful Son to earth to die in our place, that we might live with Him forever in heaven.

Now, that's *strange*.

I think author Chuck Swindoll hit the nail on the head when he wrote, "Jesus' return will be the absolute greatest surprise. Well, maybe I had better not say *that*. The *greatest* surprise is that people like us will be included in the group, stunned and dumb with wonder. That won't be just a surprise or a dream. That'll be a flat-out miracle."[1]

Call it a surprise, a dream, a wonder, or just plain strange, the fact is that the Holy God of the universe loves us, warts and all. He loves us not out of duty, not out of pity, not even out of morbid curiosity. As He told the Israelites in Deuteronomy 7:7–8, He loves us because He loves us. It's His nature.

And that, friends, isn't strange at all — it's wonderful beyond description. So wonderful that it will take us all eternity to appreciate the depth of that awesome wonder.

endnotes

Chapter 1

1 Herbert Schlossberg, *Called to Suffer, Called to Triumph* (Portland, OR: Multnomah Press, 1990), p. 151–152.

2 Elmer Thompson, "Views from the Americas," *Latin American Evangelist*, No. 4, p. 17.

3 George Otis Jr. and the staff of the Sentinel Group, "The Holy Spirit Around the World," *Charisma*, January 1993, p. 64.

4 Vera Mae Perkins, "How I Stayed Married for 40 Years. Part II: For Better or Worse," *Urban Family*, Winter 1993, Vol. I, No. 4, p. 21.

5 Joanne Shetler with Patricia Purvis, *And the Word Came with Power* (Porltand, OR: Multnomah Press, 1992), p. 15–17.

Chapter 2

1 D.A. Carson in *The Expositor's Bible Commentary, Volume 8*, general editor Frank E. Gaebelein (Grand Rapids, MI: Zondervan Publishing House, 1984), p. 392.

2 Walter Liefeld in *The Expositor's Bible Commentary, Volume 8*, general editor Frank E. Gaebelein (Grand Rapids, MI: Zondervan Publishing House, 1984), p. 994.

3 Ibid., p. 703.

Chapter 3

1 "*Glasnost*, Yeltsin, and Billy Graham — Odd Things Are Happening in U.S.S.R." *World*, No. 6, Vol. 12, July 27, 1991, p. 5.

2 Bill Ritchie, *Wired to Win* (Eugene, OR: Harvest House Publishers, 1993).

3 This account based on Philip Schaff, *History of the Christian Church, Vol. VII,* "Modern Christianity: The German Reformation" (Grand Rapids, MI: Wm. B. Eerdmans Publishing Company, 1910), p. 290–332.

4 Ibid.

5 Otis et al., "The Holy Spirit around the World," p. 22.

6 Charles H. Spurgeon, *Twelve Sermons on Prayer* (Grand Rapids, MI: Baker Book House, 1971), p. 115.

Chapter 4

1 John Piper, *A Godward Life, Book Two* (Sisters, OR: Multnomah Publishers, 1999), p. 316.

2 Charlotte Allen, "The Search for a No-Frills Jesus," *The Atlantic Monthly*, December 1996; http://www.theatlantic.com/issues/96dec/jesus/jesus.htm.

3 Ibid.

4 *AFA Journal*, June 1997.
5 Joshua Sundquist in Dave and Jan Dravecky, *Portraits in Courage* (Grand Rapids, MI: Zondervan Publishing House, 1998), p. 48–49.
6 Ibid., p. 158, 160, 162.
7 "A Kid's View of Heaven," *The Encourager*, Vol. 2, No. 1, p. 4.

Chapter 5
1 Jerry White, "Leaving It in God's Hands," *Decision*, Vol. 34, No. 1, January 1993, p. 32.
2 *New Bible Dictionary*, 2nd ed. (Wheaton, IL: Tyndale House Publishers, 1982), p. 4.
3 *The Random House College Dictionary, Revised Edition* (New York: Random House, 1988), p. 968.

Chapter 6
1 Otis et al., "The Holy Spirit Around the World," p. 22.
2 Ibid., p. 22–23.
3 Ibid., p. 22.
4 Ibid., p. 21.
5 Franklin Graham, *Results for the Kingdom*, unpublished manuscript by Samaritan's Purse, August 1989.
6 "It's a Controlling Substance," *The Oregonian*, November 28, 1993, p. L10.
7 John Piper, *Desiring God* (Portland, OR: Multnomah Press, 1986), p. 26.

Chapter 7
1 Otis et al., "The Holy Spirit around the World," p. 22.
2 From a mailing sent to seminar alumni by the Institute in Basic Life Principles, "How to Experience Instant Freedom from Fear, Anger, and Depression," p. 8.
3 Otis et al., "The Holy Spirit Around the World," p. 36.
4 *The New Bible Commentary: Revised* (Grand Rapids, MI: Wm. B. Eerdmans Publishing Company, 1970), p. 412.
5 Henry Davidoff, editor, *The Pocket Book of Quotations* (New York: Pocket Books, 1952), p. 323.

Chapter 9
1 Alexander Maclaren, adapted from *The God of the Amen* (New York, Funk and Wagnalls Co., n.d.), 213, 214.
2 Otis et al., "The Holy Spirit around the World," p. 38–40.
3 Rebecca Manley Pippert, *Out of the Saltshaker and Into the World* (Downers Grove, IL: InterVarsity Press, 1979), p. 45-47.

Chapter 10
1 Colin Duriez, *The J.R.R. Tolkien Handbook* (Grand Rapids, MI: Baker Book House, 1992), p. 65.
2 Otis et al., "The Holy Spirit around the World," *p.* 36.
3 Ibid., 38.
4 Ibid.
5 This account taken from Joanne Shetler with Patricia Purvis, *And the Word Came with Power* (Portland, OR: Multnomah Press, 1992), p. 78–80, 102–103.
6 Elisabeth Elliot, *Through Gates of Splendor* (Wheaton, IL: Tyndale House Publishers, 1981), p. 257, 259, 268.
7 William P. Barker, *Who's Who in Church History* (Old Tappan, NJ: Fleming H. Revell Company, 1969), p. 146.
8 John Foxe, *Foxe's Book of Martyrs* (Springdale, PA: Whitaker House, 1981), p. 133.

Chapter 11
1 Peter King, "He Has the Strength," *Sports Illustrated*, December 14, 1992, Vol. 77, No. 25, p. 22–27.
2 Gary Smith, "As Time Runs Out," *Sports Illustrated*, January 11, 1993, Vol. 78, No. 1, p. 13–25.

Chapter 12
1 Robert Hendrickson, *The Facts on File Encyclopedia of Word and Phrase Origins* (New York: Facts on File Publications, 1987), p. 395.
2 Major General David Robinson, "Is Anyone in Charge?" *Command*, Fall 1992, Vol. 41, No. 3, p. 7.

Chapter 13
1 Charles R. Swindoll, *Growing Strong in the Seasons of Life* (Portland, OR: Multnomah Press, 1983), p. 207.